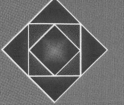

Core Science
Homework

Jean Martin and Bryan Milner

CAMBRIDGE
UNIVERSITY PRESS

Authors	Jean Martin
	Bryan Milner
Consultants	Sam Ellis
	Martyn Keeley

PUBLISHED BY THE PRESS SYNDICATE OF THE UNIVERSITY OF CAMBRIDGE
The Pitt Building, Trumpington Street, Cambridge, United Kingdom

CAMBRIDGE UNIVERSITY PRESS
The Edinburgh Building, Cambridge CB2 2RU, UK
40 West 20th Street, New York, NY 10011–4211, USA
10 Stamford Road, Oakleigh, VIC 3166, Australia
Ruiz de Alarcón 13, 28014 Madrid, Spain
Dock House, The Waterfront, Cape Town 8001, South Africa

http://www.cambridge.org

© Cambridge University Press 1999

First published 1999
Reprinted 2001

Produced by Gecko Ltd, Bicester, Oxon

Printed in the United Kingdom at the University Press, Cambridge

A catalogue record for this book is available from the British Library

ISBN 0 521 66660 0 paperback

Contents

Introduction to *Core Science Homework*

Introduction

Core Science Homework can be used both for homework assignments and as a revision aid. It may be useful for work both at home and in school.

This book contains the following features.

- Concise summaries of all the main scientific ideas pupils need to know at Key Stage 3 / ages 11 to 14 (which also makes it appropriate for those preparing for their Common Entrance Examination). These summaries are presented in short, easy-to-follow sections, each of which includes some **key words** in bold.
- Activities that focus attention on the meanings of the key words.
- Questions that require using the main scientific ideas to explain things or to solve problems.

Notes for teachers: Many of the activities are crosswords or 'fill-in-the-blanks' questions. We have tried to make it as simple as possible for these activities to be copied out into an exercise book or onto paper (plain squared graph paper would be especially useful) for completion, rather than being written in the book itself. We have included 'copy and complete' instructions with all these questions, but it is well worth re-iterating those instructions to pupils if that is the way you wish them to use the book. Alternatively, the book could be used as a one-off resource so that pupils complete the answers directly in the book.

If you are using the other *Core Science* materials as a classroom resource, you will find that the topic numbers and names are matched precisely to those used in the Basic Concepts material (whether in *Core Science 1* or in the Separate Subject editions *Core Biology, Core Chemistry* and *Core Physics*). The subject colour coding is the same too (green for biology, red for chemistry, blue for physics).

What can living things do?

Living things **feed**, **move**, **sense**, **reproduce**, **grow**, take in oxygen and get rid of waste.

oak tree   bat

owl   fly

1 Copy the grid below. Then write in the answers to the clues using the life process **bold** words. One has been done for you.

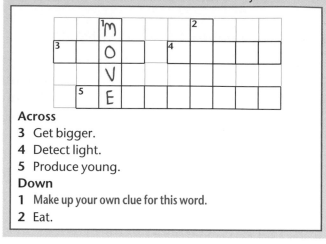

Across
3 Get bigger.
4 Detect light.
5 Produce young.
Down
1 Make up your own clue for this word.
2 Eat.

2 Read the story.

The chicks were getting bigger every day.
The mother blackbird pushed the caterpillars into their gaping mouths.
She cleaned their droppings out of the nest.

Then she flew off to look for more caterpillars.
She was breathing hard.

Copy and complete the table below.
One example has been done for you.

What the birds did	Life process
chicks produced droppings	got rid of waste

1.2 Is it alive?

Living things carry out <u>all</u> the **life processes** until they die.

Non-living things <u>might seem</u> to carry out <u>some</u> of these processes.

Non-living things are not alive and have never been alive.

1 cm

The soil in this thimble contains about a million bacteria.

1 The teacher asked Sam and Pat to write down <u>one difference between</u> living and non-living things.
Here are their answers.

Sam's answer: Living things carry out all the life processes.

Pat's answer: Living things carry out all the life processes but non-living things do not.

(a) Copy out both answers.
Draw a line under the information that is correct.
(b) Look hard at the question and explain why Sam's answer got no marks.
(c) How can you make Pat's answer better?

2 The sand in soil is non-living, but the bacteria in soil are living. Write down <u>seven</u> things bacteria do that sand doesn't.

- -

1.3 Plants are alive

Life processes are easier to see in animals than in plants. Plants make their own food so you don't see them **feed**. Land plants take in nutrients through their roots, so they can't **move** from place to place. <u>Some parts</u> move and plants can change the position of their parts when they **grow**. They can **sense** changes in their surroundings and they **reproduce** by making seeds.

1 (a) The words below are muddled up. They are five of the life processes. Unscramble them and write them in a list.

cedopurre veom worg nesse fede

(b) Now add the <u>two</u> missing life processes to your list.

2 Copy the table below.

Match each life process with the correct label from the diagram of the fly trap.

Life process	Plant organs where the life process happens
feed	
reproduce	
grow	
take in oxygen	
get rid of waste	
sense	
move	

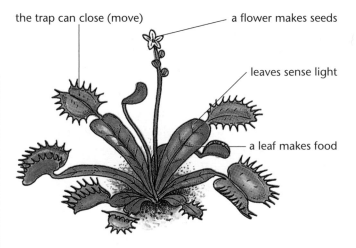

the trap can close (move)

a flower makes seeds

leaves sense light

a leaf makes food

All the parts (organs) use oxygen and get rid of waste.

1.4 Important parts of your body

Groups of **organs** make up organ systems. The organs work together to carry out life processes.

Organ system	Job or life process	Organs
digestive	breaking down food	
circulatory	transport of materials	
nervous	sense and control	

2 Look at the diagram.

(a) Write down <u>three</u> organs of the nervous system that are for sensing.

(b) Write down <u>three</u> parts of the nervous system that help to control your body.

1 Copy the table. Use the list of organs to help you to complete your copy.

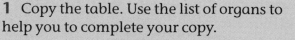

nerve   vein
large intestine   heart
brain   artery
stomach   spinal cord

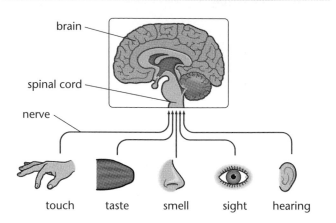

brain

spinal cord

nerve

touch   taste   smell   sight   hearing

1.5 The smallest parts of animals and plants

Animals and plants are made up of cells.

Animal cell

Plant cell

cell membrane

nucleus

cytoplasm

Plants have these extra bits.

cell wall

vacuole

cell membrane: controls what goes in and out of a cell
nucleus: controls what happens in the cell
vacuole: filled with cell sap (water, salts and sugars)
cytoplasm: where chemical reactions take place
cell wall: supports the cell and gives a cell its shape

1 Jan drew a cell 3 cm square. It had a wall lined with a cell membrane. It had a vacuole in the middle, with cytoplasm between the vacuole and the membrane. In the cytoplasm there were six small, oval, green parts and a large round nucleus.

(a) Draw a cell like Jan's. Use the **bold** words to label the parts. Next to each label, write down the job that part does.

(b) Is the cell you have drawn a plant or an animal cell?

2 Write down <u>two</u> differences between plant and animal cells.

1.6 Microbes

Microbes are everywhere but they are so small that we need a microscope to see them clearly. **Bacteria**, **viruses** and **yeast** are all microbes.

What microbes do	Example
cause disease	colds (viruses) TB (bacteria)
make useful things	bread (yeast) yogurt (bacteria)
rot and recycle waste	sewage (many kinds of microbes)

2 Look at the graph.

Which letter, A, B, C or D, marks the part of the graph where:
(a) the microbes are reproducing most rapidly?
(b) the microbes are dying faster than they are reproducing?
(c) the number of reproductions is the same as the number of deaths?

1 Copy and complete the sentences using the **bold** words.

Some microbes are harmful. For example _____ cause colds and _____ cause TB.
Other microbes are useful. We use _____ to make bread and _____ to make yogurt.

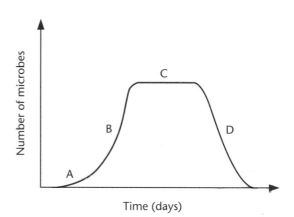
Number of microbes (y-axis), Time (days) (x-axis)

1.7 Sorting out living things

There are about 3 million different kinds of living things.
We divide them into groups. This makes it easier for us to study them. The diagram shows the three main groups. Remember we can divide each group into even smaller groups to help us sort them out.

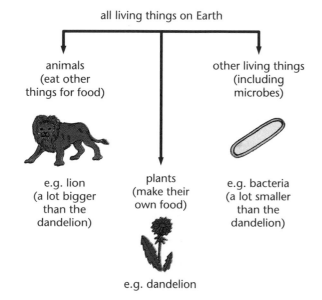

all living things on Earth

animals
(eat other things for food)

e.g. lion
(a lot bigger than the dandelion)

plants
(make their own food)

e.g. dandelion

other living things
(including microbes)

e.g. bacteria
(a lot smaller than the dandelion)

1 (a) Write the letters of the alphabet in a list. Add the name of one living thing for as many of the letters as you can.
(b) Draw a ring round the names of the plants in your list.
(c) Underline the names of the microbes in your list.

You could start like this.
A Ant
B Bacterium
C Cabbage

2 (a) What makes animals different from plants? Write down as many differences as you can.
(b) What is the main difference between a plant and a microbe?
(c) We divide each main group into smaller groups. Explain why.

1.8 What is it?

When we want to find out which <u>group</u> a living thing belongs to, we can use a key. We can also use keys to find out the <u>name</u> of a living thing.

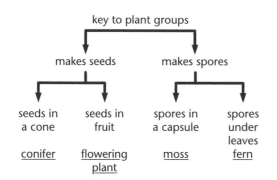

key to plant groups

makes seeds — makes spores

seeds in a cone → **conifer**

seeds in fruit → **flowering plant**

spores in a capsule → **moss**

spores under leaves → **fern**

2 If you want to grow a new lawn in your garden, you can plant grass 'seeds' in the ground. Which group of plants do grasses belong to?

A grass 'seed' is a fruit with only one seed in it.

1 On holiday in New Zealand, Ken saw these strange plants. They were a bit like trees and a bit like ferns. He used the key to find out which group they belonged to.

(a) Are these plants trees or ferns?
(b) Explain, as fully as you can, how you can use the key to find out.

fern-like leaves

cones

1.9 Sorting animals with bones

Vertebrates are animals with backbones.
We can divide them into smaller groups.

	Skin	Egg	Where egg laid	Example
fish	scales	no shell	in water	cod
amphibians	smooth, damp	no shell	in water	frog
reptiles	scales	tough shell	on land	crocodile
birds	feathers	hard shell	on land	robin
mammals	fur or hair	no shell	grows in womb	human

1 Copy the grid. Then write in the **bold** words that match the clues.

Across
4 Frogs belong to this group.
5 Our feathered friends.

Down
1 Furry animals.
2 Scaly land animals.
3 Scaly water animals.

2 From the table:

(a) write down <u>one</u> example of a reptile.
(b) write down the name of an animal which has scales and lays its eggs in water.

3 Birds and mammals have feathers or fur to keep them warm. We use feathers and down (tiny fluffy feathers) to make duvets. Design a test to find out which kind of feather is best for keeping the heat in.

1.10 Sorting animals that don't have bones

Animals without bones are called invertebrates.

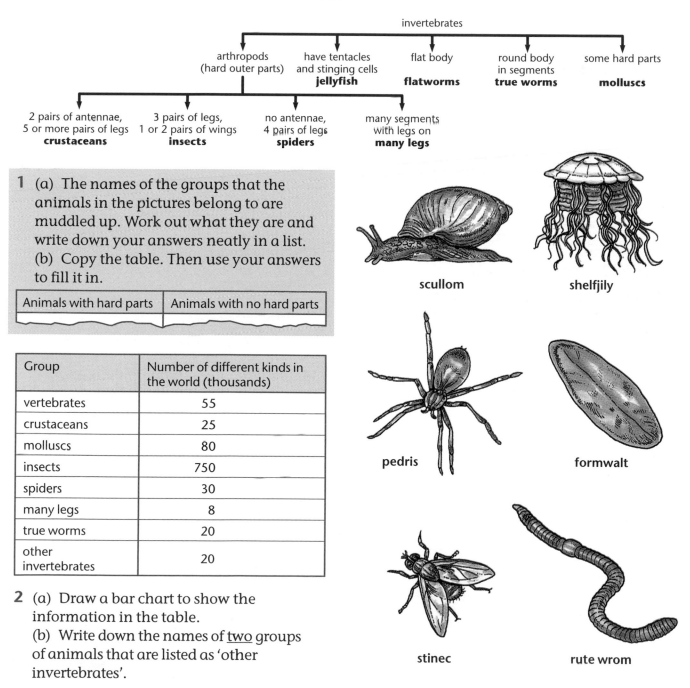

1 (a) The names of the groups that the animals in the pictures belong to are muddled up. Work out what they are and write down your answers neatly in a list.
(b) Copy the table. Then use your answers to fill it in.

Animals with hard parts	Animals with no hard parts

Group	Number of different kinds in the world (thousands)
vertebrates	55
crustaceans	25
molluscs	80
insects	750
spiders	30
many legs	8
true worms	20
other invertebrates	20

2 (a) Draw a bar chart to show the information in the table.
(b) Write down the names of <u>two</u> groups of animals that are listed as 'other invertebrates'.

2.1 Healthy eating

For a healthy **diet**, you need to eat the right types of food.

You need:

plenty of	not too much
● **proteins**	● **fat**
● **vitamins** (A, B, C, D etc.)	● sugar
● **minerals** (calcium, iron etc.)	● salt
● **fibre**	

2 Fats are energy foods.

(a) Some people need to eat food with lots of fat in. What sort of person needs to eat a high fat diet to stay healthy? Explain your answer.

(b) Other people need to eat low fat diets. Use food labels to find out the amount of fat in six foods. Write them down in order starting with the lowest fat food.

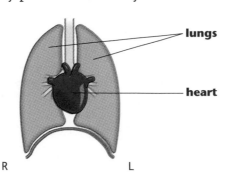

1 Copy the grid below.
Then write in the **bold** words that match the clues. One has been done for you.

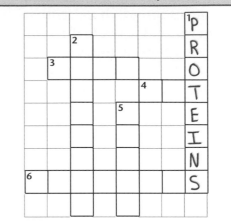

Across
3 Word for the food that you eat.
4 Don't eat too much of this.
6 Calcium is one of these.

Down
1 Make up your own clue for this word.
2 Letters identify these.
5 This prevents constipation.

Some people need lots of energy foods for keeping warm.

2.2 Born to exercise

In science, we often need to study diagrams of parts of the body. They are always drawn in front view. So, the right-hand side of a person's body part is shown on your left.

this is the right-hand side of the body part

lungs

heart

R   L

1 Copy the grid. Then write in the **bold** words from both diagrams for this section that match the clues. If your answers are correct, the word in the green box will also be a bold word.

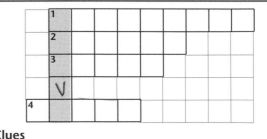

Clues
1 One of the thick-walled parts of your heart.
2 One of the upper spaces of your heart.
3 Where blood gets oxygen.
4 A pump for blood.
Make up your own clue for the word in the green box.

2 (a) Make a large copy of the diagram of the heart.
Colour in the muscular wall of the heart.
(b) Add the words 'left' or 'right' to the labels in the boxes.
(c) Heart valves stop blood flowing the wrong way. Label the other heart valve.
(d) Draw arrows to show the direction of blood flow between the atrium and ventricle on each side of the heart.

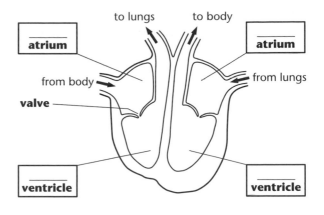

Where does blood travel?

Blood circulates around your body.
It carries substances such as glucose and oxygen.

Veins:
- the 'vé in' (way in) to the heart
- thin walls
- valves to stop blood going the wrong way

Arteries:
- carry blood from the heart (way 'art'/out)
- thick muscular walls
- no valves

Capillaries:
- very narrow tubes
- every cell is near to one
- walls one cell thick to let substances in and out

1 Make a large copy of the diagram above.

(a) Label the diagram using the **bold** words.
(b) Slices across arteries, veins and capillaries look different. Which of the diagrams below is which?

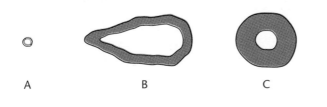

A   B   C

2 The table below shows Mia's pulse rate for different activities.

Activity	Pulse rate (beats/min)
resting	70
eating	74
walking	81
dancing	90

(a) Plot a bar chart of Mia's pulse rate.
(b) Write a sentence to say what the data tell you.

2.4 Your lungs

When you **breathe** you take <u>air</u> into and out of your lungs.

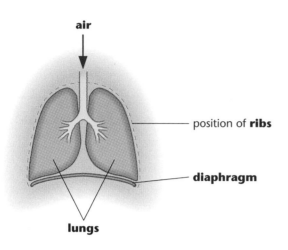

air

position of **ribs**

diaphragm

lungs

1 Copy the grid below.
Write in the **bold** words that match the clues.
If your answers are correct, the word in the green box will also be a bold word.

Clues
1 You breathe this in.
2 It separates your chest from your lower body.
3 You do this to get oxygen.
4 Where oxygen goes into your blood.
   Make up your own clue for this word.

2 The diagram above shows inside your chest when you have nearly finished breathing in. The diagram on the right shows the same parts when you have nearly finished breathing out.
Write down <u>three</u> differences between the diagrams.

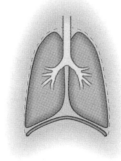

2.5 Breathing and asthma

In an asthma attack, the air pipes in the lungs get narrower. So, it is harder to get air into the air sacs. It is harder to breathe.

About 10% of children have asthma.

2 (a) Gas exchange in your lungs changes the percentages of gases in the air. Write a few sentences about the changes shown in the table.

	Air breathed in (%)	Air breathed out (%)
oxygen	21	16
carbon dioxide	0.03	4

(b) When someone stops breathing you can sometimes revive them by mouth-to-mouth resuscitation. You breathe air out of your lungs into their lungs.
Explain why this can save someone's life.

1 Look at the diagram. Then copy and complete the sentences using the **bold** words.

When you breathe, you take air into and out of your lungs. In your _____ _____,
_____ passes into your _____ and
_____ _____ passes out.
We call this _____ _____.

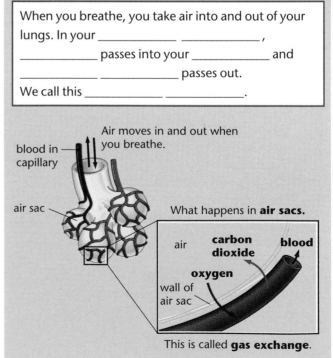

Air moves in and out when you breathe.

blood in capillary

air sac

What happens in **air sacs**.

air

carbon dioxide

blood

oxygen

wall of air sac

This is called **gas exchange**.

How do we catch diseases?

Different **microbes** cause different **diseases**. Microbes get into your body when you breathe in, when you swallow food and through cuts and natural body openings.

Fly picks up **bacteria**.

It puts bacteria on **food**.

This can cause food poisoning.

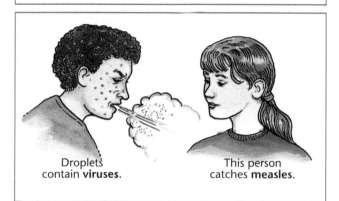

Droplets contain **viruses**.

This person catches **measles**.

2 Look at the notices. Where would you expect to see each of these notices?
Why are they put there?
(Note: you will only kill microbes in food if you make it very hot.)

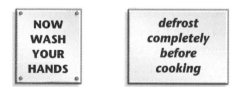

1 Copy the grid.
Write in the **bold** words that match the clues. One has been done for you.

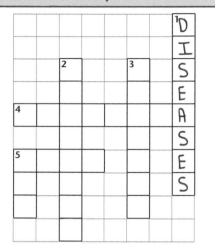

Across
4 Microbes that can cause food poisoning.
5 You may swallow bacteria with this.
Down
1 Make up your own clue for this word.
2 Microscopic living things.
3 Microbes that cause measles.
5 An insect that spreads disease.

Harmful chemicals

Drugs affect your mind and body.
They can be:
● useful or **harmful**,
● legal or illegal.

	Harmful substance	Problem
L E G A L	tobacco	causes **cancers**
	alcohol	slows reactions damages liver and brain
I L L E G A L	solvents	affect heart and brain
	LSD	makes person see things that aren't there
	cannabis	affects the mind may cause cancer

1 Look at the table. Then copy and complete the sentences using the **bold** words.

It is not against the law to use _____ and _____. But they are both _____.
Tobacco causes _____.
It is dangerous to drink and drive. It is also dangerous to use _____, _____ or _____ and drive.

2 Write down <u>five</u> questions you would ask to find out about people's smoking habits.

2.8 Long-term effects of drugs

Drugs can **damage** your body. Drugs such as **alcohol** and the **nicotine** in **tobacco** are **addictive**. Some drugs cause **cancer**.

Death rates from lung cancer.

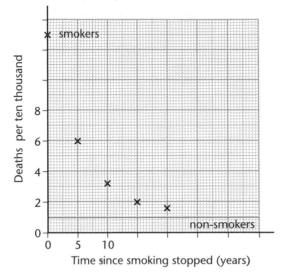

1 Copy the grid.
Write in the **bold** words that match the clues.
If your answers are correct, the word in the green box will also be a bold word.

Clues
1 The drug in beer.
2 Drugs which some people can't stop using are _____ drugs.
3 The drug in tobacco.
4 A dried leaf that people smoke.
5 What some drugs do to your body.
6 Paracetamol and penicillin are useful _____.
Make up your own clue for the word in the green box.

2 (a) Make a large copy of the graph. Complete the scales and draw a curve through the points.
(b) How many times greater is the risk to smokers than to non-smokers of dying from lung cancer?
(c) How many years after giving up smoking is the risk of lung cancer half of that for smokers?
(d) Why is it hard to give up smoking?

2.9 Your skeleton

Your skeleton supports you and protects parts of your body.
It is made of your:
- **skull**,
- **backbone**,
- **ribs**,
- shoulder girdle,
- **pelvic** girdle,
- four limbs.

Muscles pull on bones to move parts of your body. The **marrow** inside some bones makes new blood cells.

1 Copy the grid below.
Write in the **bold** words that match the clues.
If your answers are correct, the word in the green box will also be a bold word.

Clues
1 This part of bones makes blood cells.
2 Your legs fit into the _____ girdle.
3 This part protects your spinal cord.
4 This part protects your brain.
Make up your own clue for the word in the green box.

2 (a) Match the letters on the diagrams with the parts listed at the bottom of the last page.

(b) The two skeletons have the same basic plan. Write down <u>two</u> ways in which they are similar.

(c) Write down <u>two</u> differences between these skeletons.

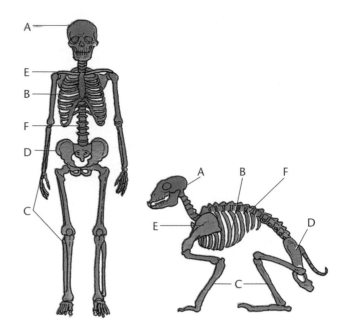

● ●

2.10 Joints

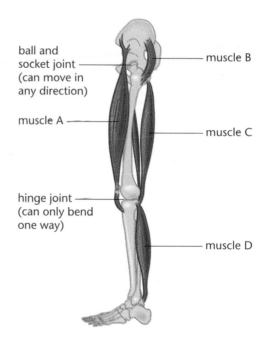

The triceps contracts to straighten the arm.
The biceps relaxes to let this happen.

1 Unscramble the words below and write them in a list.

nedtons   higen   rattccons   axelers teckos

Copy the sentences and use the unscrambled words to complete them.

> Ball and _____ joints move more than _____ joints.
>
> When your triceps _____ your biceps _____.
>
> Muscles are joined to bones by _____.

2 Muscles contract to bend and straighten your arm and your leg.

Look at the diagrams.

(a) Which muscle, A, B, C or D, contracts to bend your leg backwards at the knee?

(b) Which muscle relaxes when you bend your leg backwards at the knee?

(c) Which muscle has to contract to straighten your leg?

3.1 Fuel and energy

Food is your body's **fuel**.

food (fuel) + **oxygen** → energy

You need energy for:
- moving
- growing
- keeping warm

We measure energy in **joules** (J).
1000 joules make 1 **kilojoule** (kJ).

For growing you also need **proteins**. You get these in cereals, milk, cheese, meat and fish.

1 Copy the grid.
Write in the **bold** words that match the clues. If your answers are correct, the word in the green box will also be a bold word.

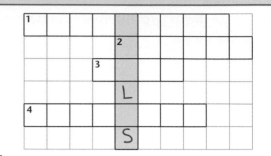

Clues

1 1000 joules = 1 _____.
2 Used to release energy from fuels.
3 Coal is a _____ that is burnt.
4 Meat and fish contain lots of these.
Make up your own clue for the word in the green box.

2 Look at the table.

(a) Who needs more energy, Ian or Bob? Why do you think this is?
(b) Why does Ian need more protein than Bob does?
(c) Both Ian and Bob need more energy from their food in the winter. Why?

	Age (years)	Energy needs (kilojoules)	Protein needs (grams)
Ian	16	15 000	100
Bob	24	13 000	64

3.2 Food for humans

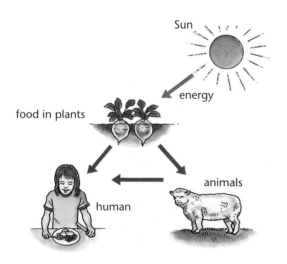

Sun
energy
food in plants
animals
human

It is often hard to tell which plant or animal our food came from. A lot of our food is changed before we get it.

1 (a) Unscramble the words and write them in a list.

degnach stapln minalas gyener

(b) Copy and complete the sentences using the words on your list.

Our food gives us the _____ and materials that we need.
It comes from _____ and from _____ which ate plants.
A lot of it is _____ before we get it.

2 Foods are energy stores. Different foods contain different amounts of energy.

(a) Which of the foods in the graph gives most energy per gram?

(b) How much energy would you get from:
- 1 g of rice?
- 100 g of carrots?

(c) What type of food are the low energy foods on this chart?

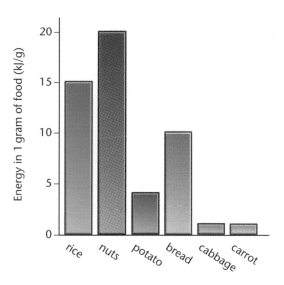

3.3 What most of your food is made of

The main things in your food are **fats**, **carbohydrates**, **proteins**, **fibre** and **water**. As the labels show, the amount of each thing varies from food to food.

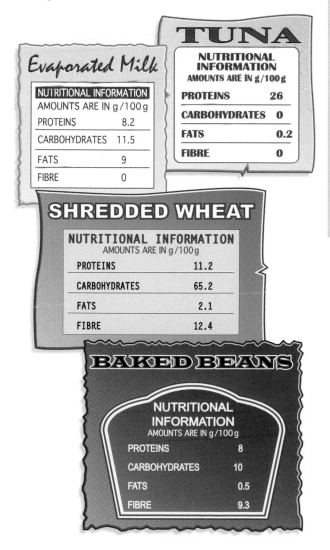

TUNA

NUTRITIONAL INFORMATION
AMOUNTS ARE IN g/100 g

PROTEINS	26
CARBOHYDRATES	0
FATS	0.2
FIBRE	0

Evaporated Milk

NUTRITIONAL INFORMATION
AMOUNTS ARE IN g/100 g

PROTEINS	8.2
CARBOHYDRATES	11.5
FATS	9
FIBRE	0

SHREDDED WHEAT

NUTRITIONAL INFORMATION
AMOUNTS ARE IN g/100 g

PROTEINS	11.2
CARBOHYDRATES	65.2
FATS	2.1
FIBRE	12.4

BAKED BEANS

NUTRITIONAL INFORMATION
AMOUNTS ARE IN g/100 g

PROTEINS	8
CARBOHYDRATES	10
FATS	0.5
FIBRE	9.3

1 Copy the grid.

Write in the **bold** words that match the clues. If your answers are correct, the word in the green box will also be a bold word.

Clues
1 There's none of this in milk.
2 Starch belongs to this group.
3 A drink from the tap.
4 Food for growth.
   Make up your own clue for the word in the green box.

2 (a) Look at the labels. Make a table to show the amount of protein in each of the foods.

(b) Colin needs a high protein, low fat diet. Which <u>one</u> of these foods should Colin avoid?

(c) Fiona needs a high fibre diet. Which <u>two</u> of these foods should Fiona eat?

(d) Why are these foods good for Colin too?

19

3.4 What else must there be in your food?

You only need small amounts of **vitamins** and minerals. But you can't stay healthy without them.

Vitamin or mineral	What happens when you don't get enough
vitamin A	you can't see in dim light
vitamin C	**scurvy**
vitamin D	weak bones (rickets)
iron	not enough red blood cells
calcium	weak **bones** + teeth, cramp

1 Write a clue for each of the words in the crossword below. Use the information on the left to help you.

	¹S	²C	U	R	V	Y		³B
		A						O
		L			⁴I	R	O	N
		C						E
	⁵V	I	T	A	M	I	N	S
		U						
		M						

2 Terry and Kiran were testing the idea that boiling destroys vitamin C. They used a purple solution that loses its colour with vitamin C.

$$\text{purple solution} \xrightarrow{\text{vitamin C}} \text{colourless}$$

The diagram shows their test tubes after they had added 10 drops of juice to the dye.

Terry said that the boiled juice had more vitamin C than the fresh juice.
Kiran said that wasn't true because the test wasn't fair.

Write down <u>three</u> things that would make it a fair test.

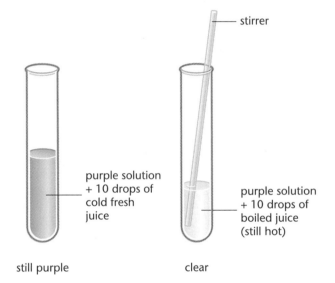

stirrer

purple solution + 10 drops of cold fresh juice

still purple

purple solution + 10 drops of boiled juice (still hot)

clear

3.5 Where does your food go?

1 (a) Make a list, in order, of the parts that food goes through on its way from the mouth to the anus.
Use <u>all</u> the **bold** words.
(b) Make up a rap to describe this journey. You could start like this:

Teeth for a good chew
That's not hard to swallow …

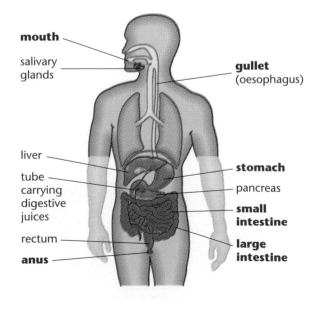

mouth

salivary glands

gullet (oesophagus)

liver

tube carrying digestive juices

rectum

anus

stomach

pancreas

small intestine

large intestine

2 (a) What do we call the kinds of juices that the salivary glands and stomach make?
(b) Write down <u>two</u> other parts of the body which make these kinds of juices.
(c) These juices contain chemicals called enzymes that digest food. Baby Joanna has digestive glands that are not very good at making enzymes. How do you think that this will affect her as she grows up?

3.6 Digesting your food

1 Look at the diagram. Then copy and complete the sentences using the **bold** words.

Even small pieces of food contain large _____.
_____ break down large molecules into small molecules. These are _____ and can pass into the _____.
Different enzymes break different _____ _____.

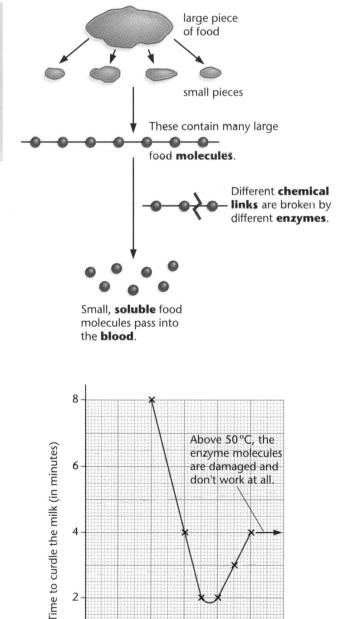

large piece of food

small pieces

These contain many large food **molecules**.

Different **chemical links** are broken by different **enzymes**.

Small, **soluble** food molecules pass into the **blood**.

2 Babies make an enzyme in their stomach that curdles milk.
The graph shows the results of an experiment to find out the effect of temperature on this enzyme.

(a) At which temperatures does the enzyme work fastest?
(b) How long did it take for the milk to curdle:
    (i) at 20 °C
    (ii) at 45 °C?
(c) A tube of milk and enzyme is kept at 65 °C. The temperature is then lowered to 35 °C. What will happen now to the milk? Explain your answer.

Above 50 °C, the enzyme molecules are damaged and don't work at all.

Time to curdle the milk (in minutes)

Temperature (°C)

3.7 Absorbing and using food

The flow diagram shows what happens to food and oxygen in your body.

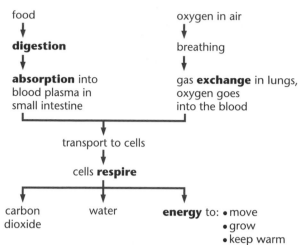

1 Copy and complete the sentences using the **bold** words to fill in the blanks.

We call the breakdown of large food molecules _____. We call taking substances into the blood _____. Gas _____ happens in the lungs. All living cells release _____ from food when they _____.

2 Use both diagrams to help you write about what is happening at arrows A, B, C and D. Write one sentence for each letter.

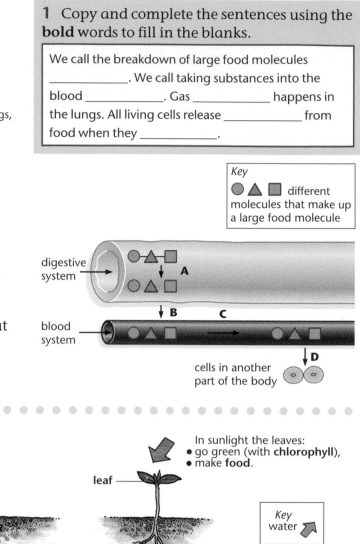

Key
◯ △ ▢ different molecules that make up a large food molecule

3.8 How do plants grow?

In sunlight the leaves:
• go green (with **chlorophyll**),
• make **food**.

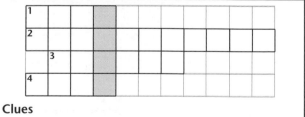

A packet of dry seeds.

A **seed** uses **stored** food at first to grow.

A seedling makes its own food.

Key
water ➚

1 Copy the grid.
Write in the **bold** words that match the clues. If your answers are correct, the word in the green box will also be a bold word.

 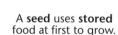

Clues
1 Green plant organ.
2 Green substance in a plant.
3 Food is _____ in a seed.
4 A new plant grows from this.
   Make up your own clue for the word in the green box.

2 Judy kneels on a mat when she weeds the garden. Last time she forgot to pick the mat up. Two weeks later she saw tiny green weed seedlings all round the mat. The seedlings underneath the mat were pale yellow.

(a) What did the seedlings grow from?
(b) Explain why some of the seedlings were green and others were pale yellow.
(c) Why don't seeds grow in their packets?

3.9 Minerals for plant growth

Element	Why it is needed	Shortage of element means
nitrogen (N)	to make proteins	leaves are yellow
phosphorus (P)	to make proteins and chemicals for energy release, root growth	leaves are dull with brown edges
potassium (K)	cell division, flower + fruit growth	leaves have yellow edges

To **grow** well, plants take in certain elements through their roots.

1 Copy and complete the sentences using the **bold** words.

> Plants need elements such as _____ (N), _____ (P) and _____ (K). If plants are short of these elements they can't _____ properly.

2 Look at the pictures.

(a) Describe the healthy plant (plant A) grown in the complete culture solution.
(b) Describe the differences between the healthy plant and plants B, C and D.
(c) Which mineral does each plant lack? Look back at the table for help.

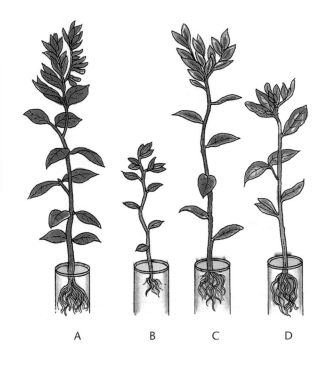

A   B   C   D

3.10 How plants take in what they need

1 Copy the table. Complete it using the **bold** words from the diagram.

What a plant needs to make food	Where it takes it in

2 Plants make food in chloroplasts. Some cells have more chloroplasts than others.

(a) Copy the table.

Number	Layer A	Layer B
cells		
chloroplasts		

In the diagram count the number of cells and chloroplasts in layer A, then in layer B of the leaf. Write the numbers in your table.
(b) In which layer of a leaf is most food made? Explain your answer.

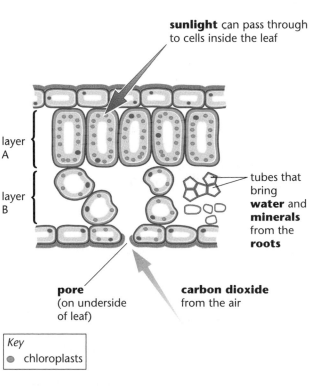

sunlight can pass through to cells inside the leaf

layer A

layer B

tubes that bring **water** and **minerals** from the **roots**

pore (on underside of leaf)

carbon dioxide from the air

Key
● chloroplasts

*Slice across a **leaf**.*

4.1 Making babies

In human **reproduction**, male and female
sex cells join in a process called **fertilisation**.

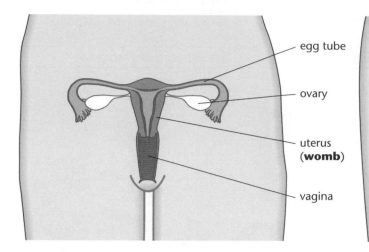

Female reproductive organs.

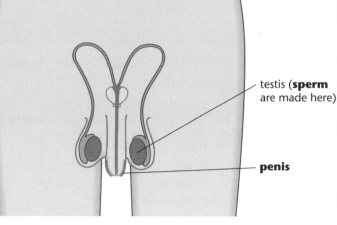

Male reproductive organs.

1 Copy the grid below.
Write in the **bold** words that match the clues.
If your answers are correct, the word in the
green box will also be a bold word.

		1							
		2							
	3								
4									
5									

Clues
1 A name for sperm and egg cells (two words).
2 Used to put sperm into the vagina.
3 Life process of having young.
4 Name for joining of egg and sperm.
5 Another name for the uterus.
   Make up your own clue for the word in the green box.

2 (a) Copy the diagrams above and label
the parts.
(b) Colour blue the parts which make
sperm cells.
(c) Colour red the parts which make
egg cells.
(d) Underline the name of the part where
fertilisation happens.
(e) Draw a ring round the name of the
part where the baby develops.

4.2 Growing and changing

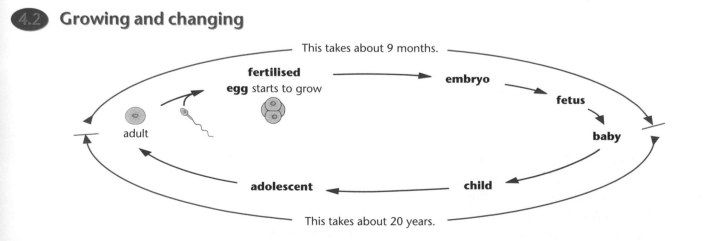

1 Copy the flow chart. Then fill in the boxes using the **bold** words from the diagram at the bottom of the last page.

2 (a) Humans look after their children for a long time. Parents have to do lots of things for their children. Write down the <u>five</u> most important things that they do.
(b) Write a few sentences about the ways in which the knowledge and experience of grandparents can help parents.

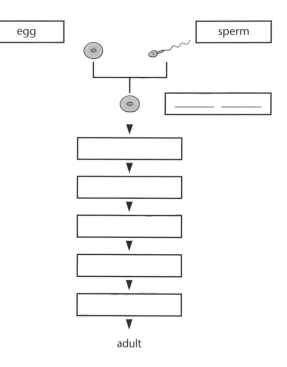

4.3 Growing pains

Our bodies change as we grow up.
The table describes some of these changes.

Some changes during **puberty**	
Girls	Boys
hair grows under **arms**	hair grows under arms
pubic hair grows	pubic hair grows
ovaries start to release **sex cells** (eggs)	testes start to release sex cells (sperm)
monthly **periods** begin	**voice** deepens

1 Copy the sentences. Then complete them using the **bold** words.

Boys and girls start to make _____
_____ at _____. They grow _____
_____ and hair under their _____.
A boy's _____ deepens and a girl starts to have monthly _____.

2 Look at the graph.

(a) During which year of life is growth rate fastest?
(b) Describe the changes in growth rate as a child grows older.
(c) Copy the part of the graph from 10–17 years.
Boys start their growth spurt later than girls but then they grow faster. Draw bars in a different colour on your graph where you think they should be for boys.
(d) Growing up brings problems for boys and girls. Write a letter to the 'Problem Page' of a teenage magazine about <u>one</u> of the problems of growing up.
Then imagine that you are the 'Agony Aunt'. Write her reply.

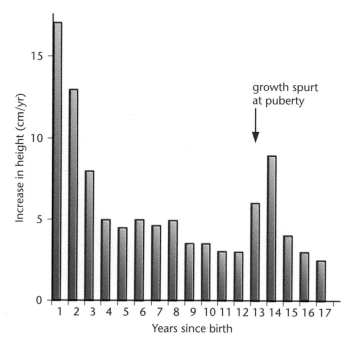

How fast an average girl grows.

`25`

4.4 A new plant life

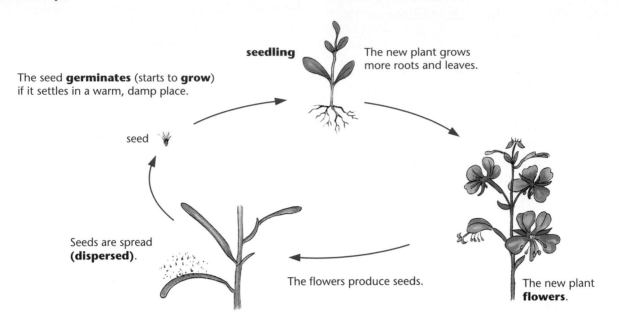

seedling — The new plant grows more roots and leaves.

The seed **germinates** (starts to **grow**) if it settles in a warm, damp place.

seed

Seeds are spread **(dispersed)**.

The flowers produce seeds.

The new plant **flowers**.

The life cycle of a flowering plant.

1 Unscramble the words in the brackets. Then write out the sentences in the correct order.

The seeds are spread or [predissed].
The [lisdegen] grows.
The [woflers] make seeds.
A seed starts to grow [minerstage].
Flowers [worg].

2 (a) How do you think that this seed is spread? Write down a reason for your answer.

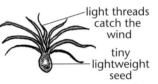

light threads catch the wind

tiny lightweight seed

(b) Plants make lots of seeds. Most of them don't grow into new plants. Write down <u>two</u> other things that can happen to seeds to stop them growing into plants.

4.5 Looking at a plant's sex organs

Flowers are a plant's reproductive system.

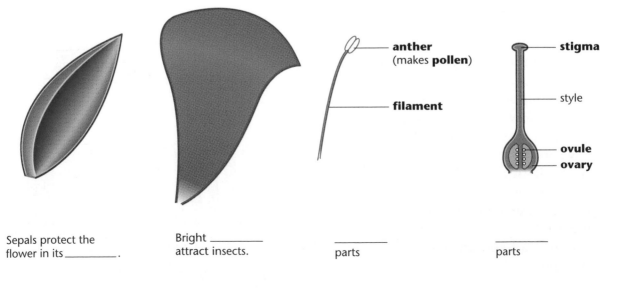

anther (makes **pollen**)

filament

stigma

style

ovule
ovary

Sepals protect the flower in its _____.

Bright _____ attract insects.

_____ parts

_____ parts

1 Copy the grid.
Write in the **bold** words that match the clues.
If your answers are correct, the word in the green box will also be a bold word.

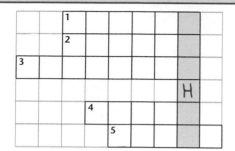

Clues
1 Pollen lands here in pollination.
2 Contains male sex cells.
3 Supports the anther.
4 Contains a female sex cell.
5 Where ovules are.
Make up your own clue for the word in the green box.

2 (a) Copy the drawings at the bottom of page 26. Copy the labels and complete them using the words in this list.

bud
female
male
petals

(b) Colour the part that makes pollen in yellow.
(c) Colour the ovules red.

4.6 Making seeds

A male sex cell is inside a **pollen** grain. It cannot move to a female sex cell by itself. Pollen is usually carried from the **anther** to the **stigma** by an **insect** or by the **wind**. When pollen lands on the stigma of a flower of the same kind, we call this **pollination**.

1 Copy the diagram. Use the **bold** words to fill in the blanks.

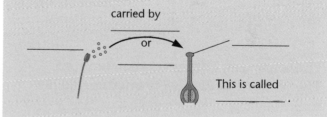

carried by

_____ or _____

This is called _____.

2 Look at the diagrams.
Copy and complete the flow chart to show the journey of a male sex cell between pollination and fertilisation.

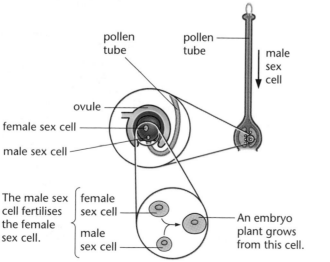

pollen tube   pollen tube   male sex cell

ovule

female sex cell

male sex cell

The male sex cell fertilises the female sex cell.   female sex cell   male sex cell   An embryo plant grows from this cell.

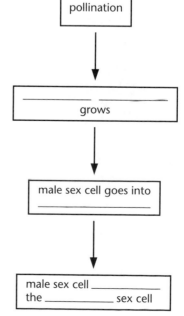

pollination

↓

_____ grows

↓

male sex cell goes into _____

↓

male sex cell _____ the _____ sex cell

4.7 What is a species?

We call each different kind of plant and animal a **species**. Members of a species are **similar**. They can **interbreed** and produce **fertile** offspring.

1 The caption on the picture has been torn.

(a) Copy and complete the caption using the **bold** words.
(b) Underline the word which means breed with each other.
(c) Draw a ring round the word which means able to reproduce.

rabbit

hare

Rabbits and hares are simi
But they are different spe
So, they cannot interbre
and produce fert
offspring.

2 A gardener pollinated the flowers on one bean plant with pollen from a different bean plant.

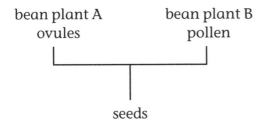

bean plant A   bean plant B
    ovules   pollen

seeds

The seeds were harvested, then planted. The plants that grew were infertile (did not make seeds).

Were beans A and B the same species? Explain your answer.

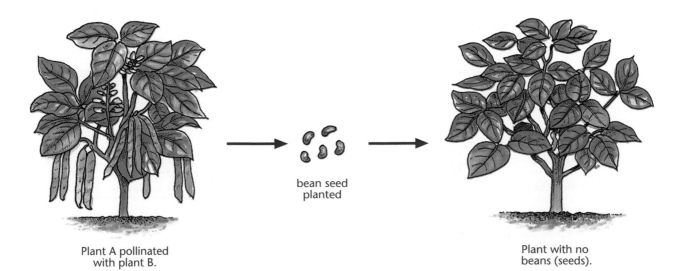

Plant A pollinated   bean seed   Plant with no
with plant B.   planted   beans (seeds).

4.8 We are all different

Humans belong to the **same species**. But they have different **features** or characteristics. We say that they **vary**.
Other plants and animals also vary.

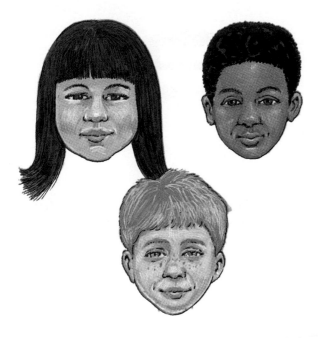

1 Copy the grid.
Write in the **bold** words that match the clues below. If your answers are correct the word in the green box will also be a bold word.

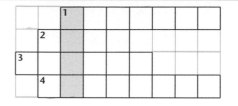

Clues
1 Rabbits and hares are different _____.
2 We are all different. We say that we _____.
3 You belong to this species.
4 Another word for characteristics.
   Make up your own clue for the word in the green box.

2 The petal length of Nicotiana flowers varies. The bar chart shows this. Use the bar chart to answer the questions.

(a) What is the most common petal length?
(b) How many flowers have petals of this length?
(c) The <u>range</u> is the difference between the shortest and longest petals.
What size are the shortest petals?
What size are the longest petals?
What is the range?

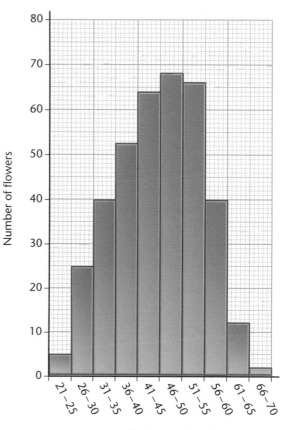

Length of petals (mm)

5.1 Night-time and day-time animals

The temperature and amount of light vary between day and night.

Different animals feed at different times. They are adapted to find food at these times.

Adapted to feed	
during the day	between dusk + dawn
sparrow	bat
kestrel	owl

2 Nocturnal animals feed between dusk and dawn.

(a) Write down the names of <u>two</u> nocturnal animals.

(b) Bats and owls find food using their ears, but kestrels and sparrows find food using their eyes. Explain why.

1 Copy the diagram. Use words from the list to complete it.

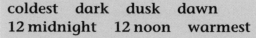

coldest   dark   dusk   dawn
12 midnight   12 noon   warmest

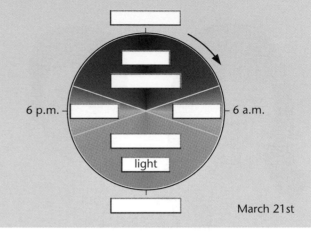

6 p.m.   6 a.m.

light

March 21st

5.2 How animals and plants survive the winter

The **shortest, coldest** days are in **winter**. **Summer** has the **warmest, longest** days.

Plants and animals are adapted to survive the changing seasons. There are times when plants do not feed and grow. Animals are adapted in different ways. They can:

- stay active,
- hibernate,
- migrate.

1 Copy the diagram of the seasons. Complete it using the **bold** words.

_____ days

spring

autumn

_____ days

2 Some butterflies, such as the Painted Lady, migrate from Britain to warmer places for the winter. Others, such as the cabbage white, hibernate. Different species hibernate at different stages in their life cycle.

(a) Draw a bar chart of the information in the table.

(b) For each pair of words below, write a sentence that links them.

(autumn / migrate)
(hibernate / winter)

Butterflies can hibernate as	Number of species that do this
eggs	9
larvae (caterpillars)	35
pupae	11
adults	7

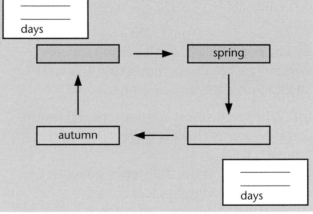

Number of species

What butterflies hibernate as

5.3 **Town and country**

The place where a plant or animal lives is called its habitat. Different plants and animals live in different habitats.

1 Copy the sentence below. Unscramble the words and use them to fill the blanks.

espac   thelers   dofo

| An animal's habitat provides the _____, _____ and _____ that it needs. |

2 (a) Match up the animals and plants in the pictures with their habitats.
(b) Write down <u>one</u> reason why a cave is not a good habitat for a plant.
(c) Describe <u>two</u> problems of living in a desert habitat.

cactus

pond

bat

desert

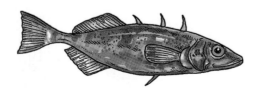

stickleback

cave

5.4 Different bodies for different habitats

Plants and animals are **adapted** to **survive** in their **habitats**.

Land animals and plants have more supporting tissue than water animals and plants. This is because water gives some **support**. Animals need to **move**. They have different adaptations for movement in different habitats.

Wings are useful for flying.

Legs are useful for moving on land.

1 Copy the grid.
Write in the **bold** words that match the clues. One has been done for you.

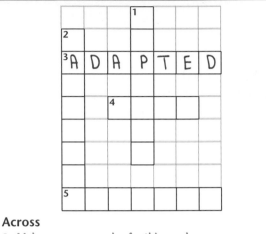

Across
3 Make up your own clue for this word.
4 Change position.
5 Stay alive.
Down
1 Hold up.
2 Places to live.

2 Copy the sentences. Then use words from the list to fill in the blanks.

bladder   tail   steering

The fish is adapted for moving in water. It has:
- strong _____ muscles for swimming.
- fins for _____ and stopping.
- a swim _____ so that it doesn't sink to the sea bed.

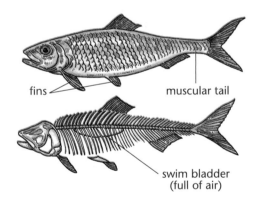

fins   muscular tail

swim bladder
(full of air)

5.5 Surviving in a garden

Plants and animals are adapted to get food and oxygen in different ways.

1 Copy the sentences. Then use the information from the pictures to complete them.

These insects are adapted to feed on _____. They suck it up through a _____ which is a bit like a drinking straw. The _____ can feed on flowers A and B. The _____ can feed only on flower A. When it is not feeding, the butterfly's proboscis is _____.

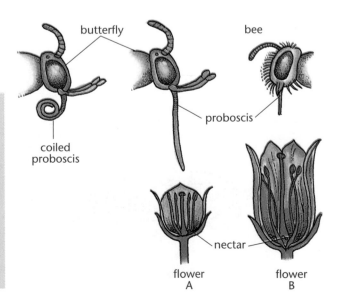

butterfly   bee

proboscis

coiled
proboscis

nectar

flower   flower
A   B

2 Fish are adapted to get oxygen from the water. They take water in through their mouths and across their gills. There are lots of blood capillaries in the gills. Oxygen passes from the water into the blood.

(a) Describe the shape of a gill filament.
(b) What job does the blood in the gills do?
(c) Why are gills good at doing this job?

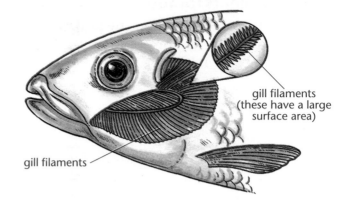

gill filaments
(these have a large
surface area)

gill filaments

5.6 Feeding on plants

Food chains show what eats what.

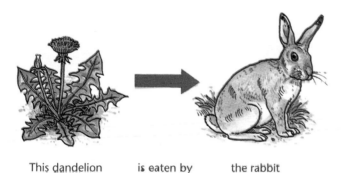

This dandelion   is eaten by   the rabbit   that is eaten by   the fox.

Food chains begin with green plants. This is because only green plants <u>make</u> food. Food (and energy) pass along the food chain.

1 (a) The pictures show the animals that Simon found in the leaf litter in a wood. Make <u>two</u> food chains with at least <u>three</u> living things in each.
(b) These food chains start with dead leaves. Other food chains start with nuts or with nectar. But we say that <u>all</u> food chains begin with green plants. Why can we still say this?

woodlouse   millipede

These animals feed on dead leaves.

2 A female mosquito fed on my blood and flew off. A swift swooped down and swallowed the mosquito. The swift was eaten by a hawk.

(a) Write out a food chain for this story.
(b) Your answer to part (a) is not a complete food chain.
  (i) Explain why.
  (ii) Make it into a complete food chain.
(c) Make up a food chain story of your own.

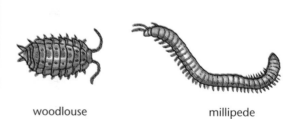

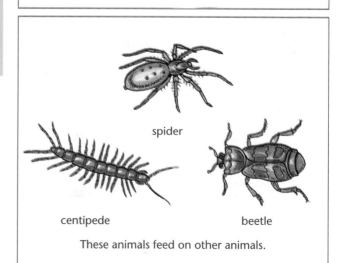

spider

centipede   beetle

These animals feed on other animals.

5.7 Growing plants for food

Many farmers and gardeners use **pesticides** to control or kill pests. Some use a **predator** that eats the pest as its **prey**.

2 Killing pests with pesticides is called <u>chemical</u> control. Using predators is called <u>biological</u> control.
Explain these names.

3 Growing plants for crops takes money, time and effort. It is important to harvest as much of a crop as possible.

(a) Look at the diagram. What percentage of our crops, on average, do we harvest in Europe?
(b) Describe <u>two</u> kinds of damage that pests do to fruit and vegetables.
(c) Organic farmers don't use pesticide sprays to kill pests and prevent this damage. Some people prefer unsprayed fruit and vegetables even if they are slightly damaged. Explain why.

1 Copy and complete the sentences. All the missing words start with the letter p.

Whitefly damage plants in greenhouses.
Some gardeners use chemicals called _____ to kill them.
Others use a _____ that kills and eats them.
The whitefly are their _____.

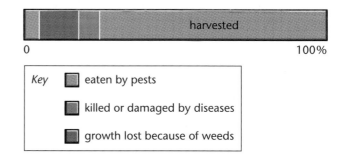

harvested

0   100%

Key	eaten by pests
	killed or damaged by diseases
	growth lost because of weeds

Slugs eat large holes in potatoes.

Blackfly feed on the sap of this bean plant. Less of the plant's food will be used for growing beans.

5.8 Predators, harmful and useful

A predator kills and eats other animals. The animals that it eats are its prey.

The graph shows the relationship between the numbers of one kind of predator and its prey.

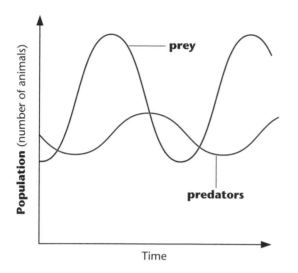

1 Copy the sentences. Then use information from the graph to help you to complete them.

> The population of its prey affects the _____ of a predator.
>
> After the number of prey increases the number of _____ also increases. Then the number of _____ goes down. So the number of _____ also goes down. This happens over and over again.

2 Look at the pictures.

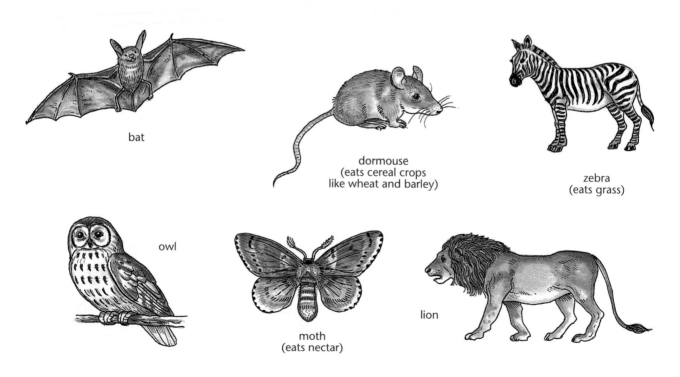

bat

dormouse
(eats cereal crops
like wheat and barley)

zebra
(eats grass)

owl

moth
(eats nectar)

lion

(a) Write down a list of the predators.
(b) Match up the predators with their prey.
(c) Draw food chains for <u>two</u> pairs. You will need to add a suitable plant to the start of each chain.
(d) Owls are useful to us. Explain why.

5.9 Garden food webs

In a habitat, plants and animals belong to more than one food chain. For example:

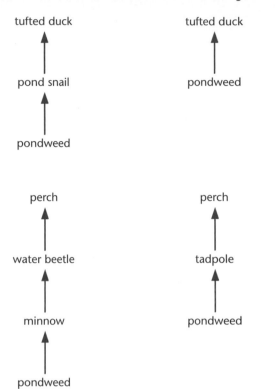

So, we join food chains to make food webs.

2 The table shows some animals and what they eat.

(a) Draw a food web for the information in the table.

(b) Humans eat crabs, whelks, periwinkles and seaweed.

Add humans to your food web.

1 Make a large copy of the food web.

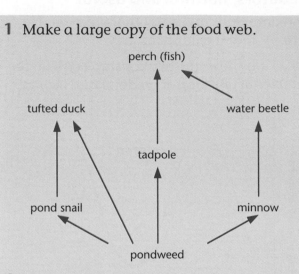

On your copy:

(a) draw a ring round the name of a plant.

(b) underline the names of <u>two</u> predators.

(c) draw a box around the name of an animal which is both predator and prey.

(d) draw a star next to an animal which eats plants <u>and</u> other animals.

(e) write down <u>two</u> things that could happen to other animals if fishermen removed all the perch.

Animal	What it feeds on
blue-rayed limpet	brown seaweed
whelk	periwinkle
periwinkle	green seaweed
spider crab	green seaweed, periwinkle

5.10 Competition

There is a limit to the amount of space and materials that living things need.
So, animals compete for:
- **space** (territory),
- **food** and **water**,
- **mates**.

Plants compete for:
- **space** (to settle),
- **minerals** and **water**,
- **light**.

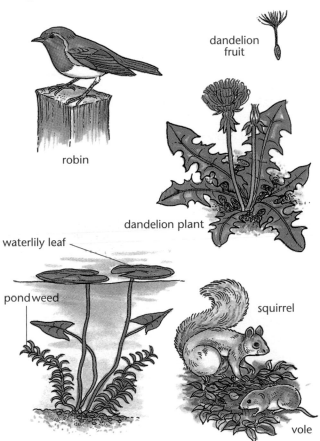

dandelion
fruit

robin

dandelion plant

waterlily leaf

pondweed

squirrel

vole

1 (a) Copy the sentences. Then use the **bold** words to complete them.

> Male robins singing on fence posts are competing for _____.
>
> Dandelion seeds landing on a lawn are competing for _____.
>
> Waterlily leaves floating above pondweed are competing for _____.
>
> A dandelion plant growing on a lawn is competing for _____ and _____
>
> Squirrels and voles searching for nuts are competing for _____.

(b) Add to your answers:
- a tick if the animal or plant is competing with its own species,
- a star if it is competing with other species.

(Note: you can use a tick and a star for the same living thing.)
Add a key to show what the tick and the star mean.

2 The ground under rhododendrons is so shaded that other plants cannot grow there. Scientists think that poisonous substances leak out of the roots of rhododendrons into the soil. These poisons also stop other plants growing.

How could you find out if the soil under rhododendrons does affect other plants?

Make sure that you say:
- where you take soil samples from,
- what you grow in the soil,
- how you would make the test fair,
- what results you would expect.

POISON

1.1 The right one for the job

Different materials have different **properties**.

For example:

- materials that let an electric current flow through them easily are called <u>electrical conductors</u>;
- materials that let thermal energy pass through them easily are called <u>thermal conductors</u>;
  (Note: In everyday life, people often use the word 'heat' to mean thermal energy.)
- materials that are very poor thermal or electrical conductors are called **insulators**;
- you can see clearly through **transparent** materials.

2 Copy the table.
Choose the materials shown in the pictures to fill in the blanks.

Material	Property of material
_____	a good thermal conductor
1 _____ 2 _____	good thermal insulators [two of these]
1 _____ 2 _____ 3 _____	transparent [three of these]
_____	a good electrical conductor
_____	a good electrical insulator

1 Copy the grid below.
Write in the **bold** words that match the clues.
One has been done for you.
If you get the answers right, the word in the red box will be the opposite of the answer to clue 2.

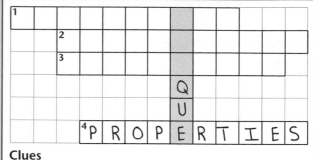

Clues

1 Metals are good thermal and electrical ____.
2 Lemonade is ____ but milk is not.
3 ____ can keep you warm or can stop shocks.
4 Make up your own clue for this word.

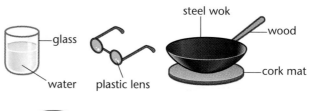

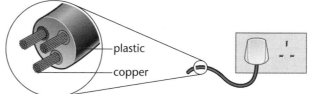

1.2 Solid, liquid and gas

Pieces of **solid** material usually stay the same **shape**.

A **liquid** changes its shape depending on what you put it in.

A **gas** will spread out to fill all the space it can.

Some substances are **denser** than others. This means that each cubic centimetre (cm^3) has a bigger mass, in grams (g) or kilograms (kg).

1 Copy the grid.
Write in the **bold** words that match the clues.

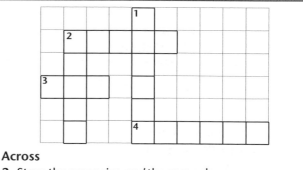

Across

2 Stays the same size *and* the same shape.
3 Spreads out everywhere it can.
4 A stone sinks because it is ____ than water.

Down

1 Fills a container from the bottom up.
2 Fixed for solids but can change for liquids.

2 Copy the sentences below.
Use information about making and burning a candle to fill in the gaps.

> You can pour molten wax into a mould because it is a _____ .
>
> The wax cools to make a candle. The wax is now a _____ so the candle stays the same _____ .
>
> The candle seems to disappear as it burns. This is because it changes into _____ .
>
> A candle floats because it is less _____ than water.

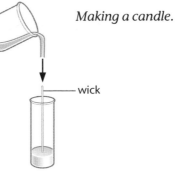

Making a candle.

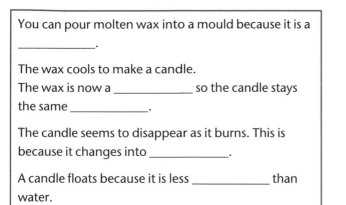

wick

Hot molten wax is poured into a mould. It fills the mould so it is the same shape.

When the wax cools, you can take the candle out of the mould.

Burning a candle.

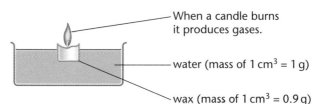

When a candle burns it produces gases.

water (mass of 1 cm³ = 1 g)

wax (mass of 1 cm³ = 0.9 g)

 1.3

Explaining the way things are

Solids, liquids and gases are all made of tiny **particles**.

Solid	**Liquid**	**Gas**

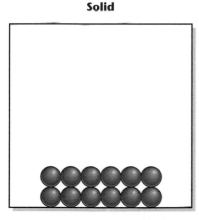 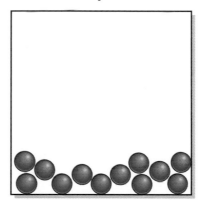 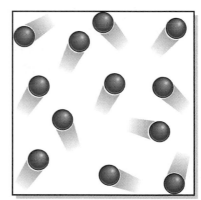

The particles are close together. They can't move around each other; they can only vibrate (wobble).

The particles can move around each other, but they all stay close together.

The particles are a long way apart. They move anywhere in the space they're in.

1 Look at the diagrams.
Use them to help you answer the following questions.

(a) You can squeeze more air into a bicycle tyre that already has plenty of air inside it. Explain why.

(b) Why <u>can't</u> you squeeze more water into a bottle that is already filled with water?

(c) Why can you pour a liquid but not a solid (unless you crush the solid and make it into a powder)?

(d) Solids and liquids are a lot denser than gases (each cm³ weighs a lot more). Why is this?

1.4 Mixing solids and liquids

When you **dissolve** a solid in a liquid you get a **solution**.

The **solid** which dissolves is called the **solute**.

The **liquid** which dissolves the solid is called the **solvent**.

1 Copy the sentences and add the missing letters to the unfinished word at the end of each line. Use the **bold** words to help you.

Salt is a ____id.
Water is a ____id.
If you mix salt with water the salt ____sol____ :
● water is the sol____,
● salt is the sol____,
● the mixture is a sol____.

2 Jo and Jez try dissolving salt in water at different temperatures.
The diagrams show their results.
Jo says that more salt dissolves in water at 10 °C than in water at 50 °C.
Jez disagrees.
He says that the test is not fair.
Write down <u>two</u> reasons why the test is not fair.

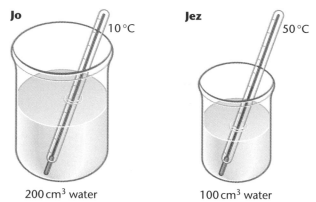

Jo 10 °C   **Jez** 50 °C

200 cm³ water
19 small spoonfuls of salt dissolve

100 cm³ water
10 small spoonfuls of salt dissolve

1.5 Melting and boiling

If you heat a **solid** it may melt into a **liquid**.
If you make the liquid hot enough it will boil.
For example, sulphur melts at 113 °C and boils at 445 °C.

The temperature at which a solid melts is called its **melting** point.

The temperature at which a liquid boils is called its **boiling** point.

1 Copy the diagram. Add the labels.
Fill in the gaps using the **bold** words.

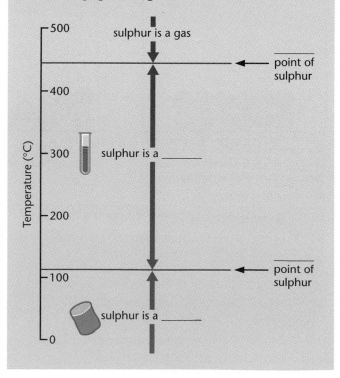

Temperature (°C)

500 — sulphur is a gas
————— point of sulphur
400
300 — sulphur is a _____
200
100 ————— point of sulphur
sulphur is a _____
0

2 Use the diagrams to help you answer the following questions.

(a) Why does the aluminium pan melt when it boils dry?
(b) Why do you think the gas flame does <u>not</u> melt the pan when there is water in it?

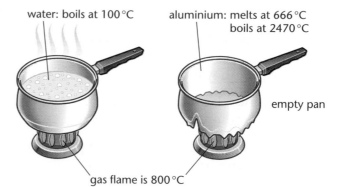

water: boils at 100 °C

aluminium: melts at 666 °C
boils at 2470 °C

empty pan

gas flame is 800 °C

1.6 Heat in, heat out

When we boil a liquid it doesn't get any hotter.
All of the **energy** that we transfer to the liquid is used to change the liquid into a gas.
A boiling liquid **evaporates** quickly.

Liquids also evaporate even if we don't heat them. They take the energy they need to evaporate from the things around them. This makes the things around them **cooler**.

To make a liquid evaporate faster you can **heat** it or **blow** air across it.

1 Copy the grid below.
Write in the **bold** words that match the clues.
One has been done for you.

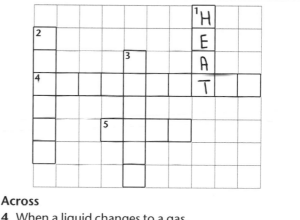

Across
4 When a liquid changes to a gas.
5 One way to speed up evaporation.
Down
1 Make up your own clue for this word.
2 Evaporation cannot happen without this.
3 Evaporation makes the surroundings ____.

2 The diagrams show five thermometers. They are all in the same room at the same time.

(a) Which three thermometers show the same temperature?
(b) Why do the other two thermometers both show a lower temperature?
(c) One of these two thermometers shows a lower temperature than the other.
Suggest a possible reason for this.

water (19 °C)

meths (19 °C)

—19 °C

air in room

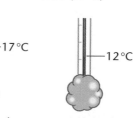

—17 °C

cotton wool
soaked in water

—12 °C

cotton wool
soaked in meths

1.7 Other effects of heating and cooling

As things become hotter they also become bigger.
We say that they **expand**.

When things are cooled they become smaller.
We say that they **contract**.

If we stop **solids** or **liquids** from expanding they produce very large **push** forces.

Gases are **squashy**. So they produce smaller forces than solids or liquids if we stop them expanding.

If we stop solids from contracting they produce very large **pull** forces.

2 The diagrams show what happens to a mercury-in-glass thermometer if you make it warmer.

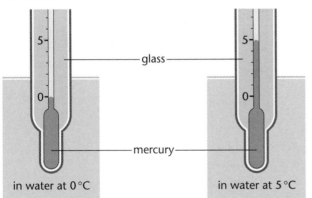

in water at 0 °C   in water at 5 °C

Choose, from the list below, the best explanation of what happens.

- The glass and the mercury both expand by the same amount.
- The mercury expands a lot more than the glass.
- Only the mercury expands.
- The mercury expands and the glass contracts.
- The glass contracts more than the mercury.

3 Look at the diagram of the ball and ring.
Copy the sentences.
Use information from the diagram to help you choose the correct red words and to fill the blanks.

> When you heat the ball, it will/won't pass through the ring.
> This is because the ball has _____.
>
> When you cool the ball, it will/won't pass through the ring.
> This is because the ball has _____.

1 Copy the grid below.
Write in the **bold** words that match the clues.
One has already been done for you.

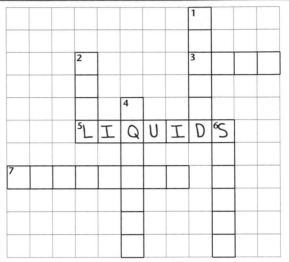

Across
3 Force produced by solids, liquids or gases if you stop them expanding.
5 Make up your own clue for this word.
7 Get smaller.

Down
1 Get bigger.
2 Force produced by a solid if you stop it contracting.
4 Gases produce smaller forces when they expand because they are ____.
6 These produce very large forces when we stop them expanding or contracting.

When the ball is cool, it *just* goes through the ring.

When the ball is hot, it *won't* go through the ring.

1.8 Looking at change

Changes happen all the time.

Many changes do <u>not</u> produce new **substances**.
We call these **physical** changes.
An example of a physical change is **evaporating** water to make steam.

Physical changes are usually easy to change back again. We say that they are easy to **reverse**.
For example, we can **condense** steam to make water again.

In <u>all</u> changes, there is the same amount of stuff before and after the change. The **mass** stays the same.

2 Sam wants to find out what happens to the mass of some salt and water when they are mixed together.
The diagrams show her results.

(a) Write down what Sam's results <u>seem</u> to show.

(b) Which of the following is most likely to be correct?

- There really is a slight increase in mass when salt dissolves in water.
- There really is a slight decrease in mass when salt dissolves in water.
- Sam spilt a little bit of the salt when she added it to the water.

1 The sentences below contain the **bold** words with the letters all muddled up.
Copy the sentences with these words sorted out.

[aaeiognprtv] water is a [aichlpsy] change because no new [aeubcnssst] are produced.
This change is easy to [eeerrsv]; all you have to do is [eeocdnns] the steam.
During these changes there is no change in [amss].

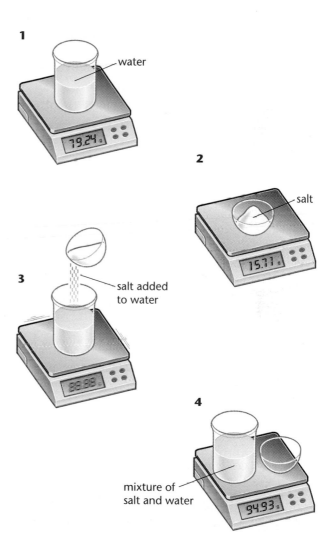

1 — water
79.24 g

2 — salt
15.71 g

3 — salt added to water
88.98 g

4 — mixture of salt and water
94.93 g

3 The table shows some other pupils' results.

(a) One pupil made a mistake when working out their result. Who was it?

(b) Leaving out the worst result:
- (i) what is the <u>total</u> difference in mass when you add all the results together (including Sam's)?
- (ii) what is the <u>average</u> difference in mass for these four results?

Name	Change in mass
Claire	0.01 g more
Jo	zero
Philip	0.01 g less
Tom	3.43 g more

2.1 Mixtures

Sea-water is a **mixture**.
It is made of ordinary **salt** and other substances dissolved in **water**.
You can get the dissolved substances out of sea-water by evaporating the water.

Air is also a mixture. It is made mainly of two gases: about $\frac{4}{5}$ is **nitrogen** and about $\frac{1}{5}$ is **oxygen**. Air also contains small amounts of other gases, such as **carbon dioxide**.

2 Milk is a mixture.
Different types of milk contain the same things mixed together in different amounts.

(a) What are full cream milk and semi-skimmed milk both mainly made of?
(b) What is the main difference between semi-skimmed milk and full cream milk?

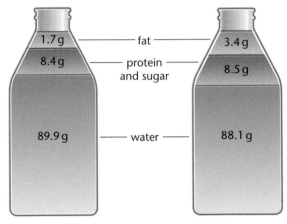

100 g semi-skimmed milk   100 g full cream milk

1 Copy the grid below.
Write in the **bold** words that match the clues.
One of them has been done for you.

Across
3 Air contains a little of this gas.
5 The sea is mainly made from ____.
6 One-fifth of the air.

Down
1 Air and water are both ____.
2 When sea-water evaporates, the substance left behind is mainly ____.
4 Make up your own clue for this word.

2.2 Taking out the bits

Liquids sometimes contain **undissolved** bits of solids.
You can remove these by **filtering**.
The bits of solid are trapped in the **filter paper**. We call these the **residue**.
The liquid that goes through the filter is called the **filtrate**.
Any solids that are **dissolved** in the liquid stay in the filtrate.

1 Copy the diagram. Add the labels.
Fill in the blanks using the **bold** words.

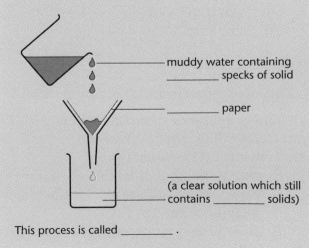

muddy water containing _____ specks of solid

_____ paper

_____ (a clear solution which still contains _____ solids)

This process is called _____ .

2 Some pupils filter some sea-water, some river water and some tap water.
They put one drop of each kind of filtered water on to a glass dish.
Then they warm the dish to evaporate the water.
The diagram shows what happened.

(a) Why did the pupils filter the water?
(b) What did the pupils find out about the amounts of dissolved solids in the three types of water?

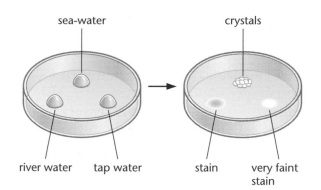

sea-water   crystals

river water   tap water   stain   very faint stain

2.3 Getting the liquid back

Water often contains **dissolved** solids.
To get pure water from a solution you must first **boil** the water.
This makes the water **evaporate** quickly.
To **condense** steam back to water you must **cool** it.
Boiling water to evaporate it and then condensing it again is called **distillation**. The pure water that is produced is called **distilled** water.

1 Copy the diagram. Add the labels.
Fill in the blanks using the **bold** words.

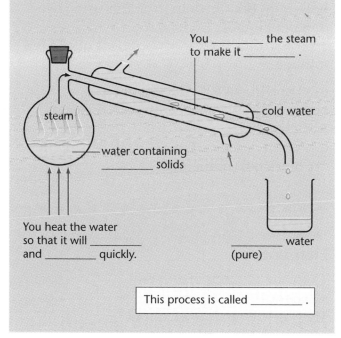

You _____ the steam to make it _____ .

cold water

steam

water containing _____ solids

You heat the water so that it will _____ and _____ quickly.

_____ water (pure)

This process is called _____ .

2 When you cook vegetables, the kitchen windows sometimes 'steam up'.

Copy the sentences and complete them to explain why this happens.

The windows 'steam up' because steam _____ on them.
The steam comes from boiling water which has _____ .
Windows steam up more in winter because the glass is _____ .

2.4 What's in a colour?

Ink is often a **mixture** of different coloured dyes.

You can separate the dyes by putting a spot of ink on to special paper.
You also need a liquid that will **dissolve** the dyes. We call this a **solvent**.

The solvent moves each dye along the paper at a different **speed**. This separates the dyes from each other.
Separating coloured dyes in this way is called **chromatography**.

1 Copy the diagrams. Add the sentences. Fill in the blanks using the **bold** words.

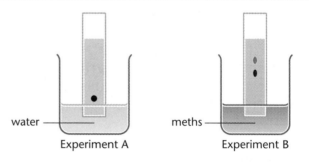

paper that soaks up the liquid

spot of green ink

Start　　　　　A few minutes later

The liquid in the beaker moves each dye up the paper at a different _____.
To do this, the liquid must _____ the dyes.
It must be a _____ for the dyes.

The green ink is a _____ of blue and yellow dyes.
This way of separating the dyes is called _____.

2 Jade wants to separate the dyes in black ball-point ink. She tries to do this using two different liquids.
The diagrams show what happens after a few minutes.

(a) Experiment B produces a good chromatogram but experiment A does not. Explain why.
(b) What does experiment B tell you about the black ball-point ink?

water

Experiment A

meths

Experiment B

2.5 Elements

There are <u>millions</u> of different substances.
They are all made from about **ninety** different substances called **elements**, joined together in different ways.

Elements can't be **split** up.
They are the **simplest** substances that there are.

Water is <u>not</u> an element because it can be split up into the elements **hydrogen** and **oxygen**.

1 Copy the grid below.
Write in the **bold** words to match the clues. One has already been done for you.

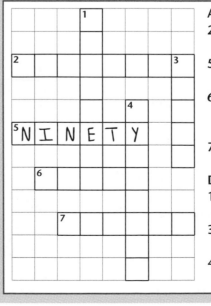

Across
2 You can't split these up into anything else.
5 Make up your own clue for this word.
6 This very common substance is not an element.
7 One of the elements in water.

Down
1 Elements are the ____ substances that exist.
3 You can't do this to an element.
4 One of the elements in water.

2 The diagram shows what happens when you heat powdered chalk.

Copy and complete the sentences.

Chalk can't be an _____ because you can split it up into _____ _____ and _____.

Chalk is made from three elements: _____, _____ and _____.

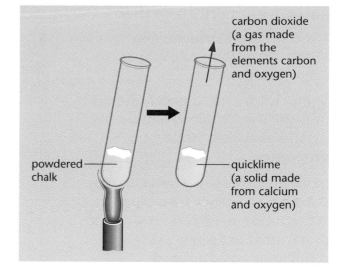

carbon dioxide (a gas made from the elements carbon and oxygen)

powdered chalk

quicklime (a solid made from calcium and oxygen)

• •

2.6 Shorthand for elements

Each element has a different symbol.

Often this is the first letter of its name. For example:

C   is the symbol for **c**arbon.

Because C is used as the symbol for carbon, the symbol for calcium has <u>two</u> letters:

Ca   is the symbol for **ca**lcium.

Sometimes the symbol for an element uses letters from an old name for an element. For example:

Na   is the symbol for **so**dium
because sodium used to be called <u>na</u>trium.

1 Copy the table.
Fill in the blanks using the **bold** words.
Unscramble the other letters to make the names of elements.

Symbol	Name of element
C	
Ca	
Cl	eiochlnr
Cu	percop
N	eiognnrt
Ne	eonn
Na	
H	eodghnry
He	eiuhlm
O	eognxy
S	uuhlprs

Here are the names of some elements to help you: chromium, copper, chlorine, hydrogen, helium, hafnium, oxygen, silicon, sulphur.

2 (a) Why is the symbol for helium He rather than H?
(b) The table shows the symbols for four elements.
Which of these elements was once called:
 (i) ferrum?
 (ii) aurum?
 (iii) kalium?
 (iv) argentum?

Symbol	Name of element
K	potassium
Fe	iron
Ag	silver
Au	gold

2.7 Putting elements together

When different elements join together they form new substances called **compounds**.

Compounds are completely different from the elements they contain. We say that they have different **properties**.

Many elements will burn in oxygen. Burning is a chemical reaction. When an **element** burns it joins with the element **oxygen** to make a compound called an **oxide**.

1 Copy the grid below.
Write in the **bold** words to match the clues. If your answers are correct, the word in the red box will also be a bold word.

						1						
						2						
3												
						D						
				4								

Clues

1 Substances made from two or more elements joined together.
2 Other elements react with this when they burn.
3 Compounds and the elements that they are made from have very different ____.
4 Oxygen is an ____.
Make up your own clue for the word in the red box.

2 Look at the diagram.
Then copy and complete the sentences by filling the blanks and choosing the correct red word.

> Hydrogen is a colourless _____.
> When hydrogen burns it reacts with _____ from the _____.
> The new substance that is produced is a compound called _____.
> This compound has completely different _____ from hydrogen and oxygen.
> For example, it is a solid/liquid/gas at 20 °C (room temperature).

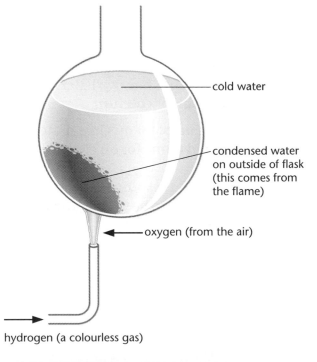

cold water

condensed water on outside of flask (this comes from the flame)

oxygen (from the air)

hydrogen (a colourless gas)

DANGER   Hydrogen and oxygen can explode. Only science teachers should do this, taking all the necessary precautions.

3 There are only about 90 elements.
So how can there be millions of different compounds?
(Hint: The information in the box should give you an idea.)

> There are only 26 letters in the alphabet:
> a b c d e f g h i j k l m n o p q r s t u v w x y z
>
> These letters are joined together in **lots** of different ways, for example:
>   the these see their hire
>
> So there are thousands of different words.

2.8 Useful compounds

Two compounds that we often <u>use</u> in everyday life are water and salt (sodium chloride).

A compound that we <u>produce</u> in everyday life is carbon dioxide.
We breathe out carbon dioxide.
We also produce it when we burn fuels such as coal, petrol, diesel fuel and charcoal. All these fuels contain carbon.

1 Copy the table.
Complete it by unscrambling the letters to make the names of elements.

Common compound	Elements it contains
water	eodghnry
	eognxy
salt	ioudms
	eiochlnr
carbon dioxide	aobcnr
	eognxy

2 Some pupils added different amounts of salt to 100 cm³ of water.
They then measured the temperature when the water froze (the freezing point) and the temperature when it boiled (the boiling point). The graphs show their results.

(a) How does adding salt change the boiling point of water?
(b) How much salt must you add to the pan of water to make it boil at:
(i) 101 °C?
(ii) 102.5 °C?
(c) Adding salt to water has a <u>different</u> effect on the freezing point than it does on the boiling point.
Write down <u>two</u> differences.
(d) How many spoonfuls of salt must you add to the pan of water so that it won't freeze until the temperature falls to:
(i) –3 °C?
(ii) –10 °C?
(e) How sure are you about each of your answers to (d)? Give reasons.

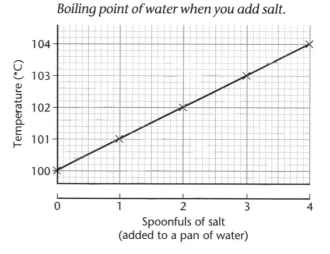

Boiling point of water when you add salt.

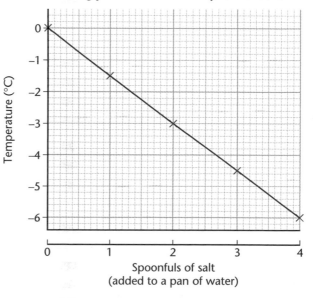

Freezing point of water when you add salt.

3 On a cold winter's day, the temperature is –6 °C.
The water in a river is frozen but the water in the sea is not.
Suggest a possible reason for this.

3.1 Looking at metals

Most metals are like each other in many ways.
We say that they have similar properties.
For example:

- they **conduct heat**,
- they **conduct electricity**,
- most are **hard**,
- most are **strong**,
- most are **tough**.

Metals are also shiny when they have just been cut but most go dull after a while.

Iron and steel are **magnetic** metals.

2 Emma tests the strength of a thin metal wire.
The diagrams show how she does this
The table shows her results.

(a) Which result should Emma ignore?
Give a reason for your answer.
(b) Why do you think one of Emma's results is so much lower than all of the others?
(c) Work out the <u>average</u> of Emma's four other results. (<u>Add</u> them up then <u>divide</u> by four.)
Write down your answer like this:

On average, the wire breaks when Emma hangs a mass of ....g on it.

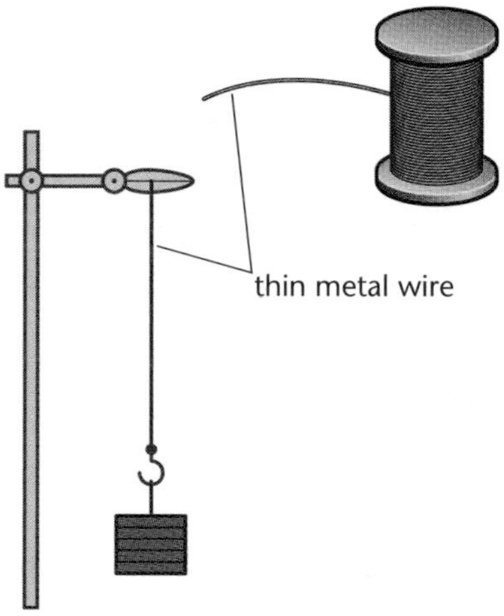

1 Copy the table.
Use the **bold** words to fill in the blanks.

Most metals ...	So we say that metals ...
don't break easily when you hit them	are _____
are not picked up by a magnet	are not _____
let electricity pass through them easily	_____ _____
don't break easily when you stretch them	are _____
let thermal energy (heat) pass through them easily	_____ _____
don't scratch or wear away easily	are _____

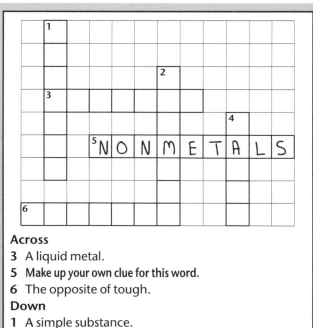

Results
(of 5 tests)

Mass needed to break wire
4200 g
4400 g
4100 g
1900 g
4100 g

thin metal wire

A sharp bend in the wire can make it weaker.

- -

3.2 Non-metals

There are about 90 simple substances.
Each simple substance is an **element**.
Most elements are metals; the others are called **non-metals**.
Solid non-metals are **brittle** and they do not usually conduct electricity.

At room temperature (20 °C):

- most metal elements and some non-metal elements are solids,
- one metal element (**mercury**) and one non-metal element (**bromine**) are liquids,
- some non-metal elements are **gases**, but no metal elements are gases.

1 Copy the grid.
Write in the **bold** words that match the clues.
One has already been done for you.

(crossword grid with 5 across reading N O N M E T A L S)

Across
3 A liquid metal.
5 Make up your own clue for this word.
6 The opposite of tough.

Down
1 A simple substance.
2 A liquid non-metal.
4 Only non-metal elements are this.

2 The diagrams show two tests on a carbon (graphite) rod.
Copy and complete the sentences by filling in the blanks and choosing the correct red word.

Test A tells you that carbon (graphite) is a
_____.
Test B tells you that carbon (graphite) conducts
_____.
This is usual/unusual for a non-metal element.

A

B

Where do we find non-metals?

Your body, the air around you and sea-water are all made mostly from non-metal elements.

Oxygen is the commonest element in our bodies (65%) and in the sea (86%).

About 20% of the air is also oxygen. This is needed for breathing and burning.

Metals make up only 3% of your body, only 1% of sea-water and 0% of the air.

You can show this information on pie charts.
If you split up a pie into 100 equal slices, each slice is 1% (1 per cent).
A bigger slice of the pie means a bigger percentage.

1 Copy the pie charts carefully.
Label and colour the parts of the pies like this:
oxygen (red)
metals (blue)
other non-metal elements (yellow)
Add a key to your charts to show what each colour means.

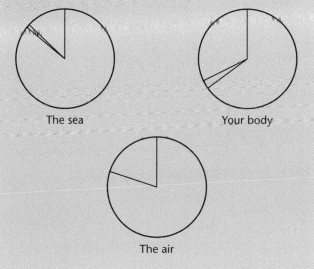

The sea   Your body

The air

2 The diagrams show an experiment about rusting. The iron filings will stick to the bottom of the tube if you wet it first.

Use the information on the diagrams to answer the questions.

(a) How much of the air is used up during rusting? Is it 10%, 20%, 50% or 100%?
(b) Which gas from the air must have reacted with the iron filings?
(c) Copy and complete the sentence.

When iron rusts it reacts with _____ to make a new substance called iron _____.

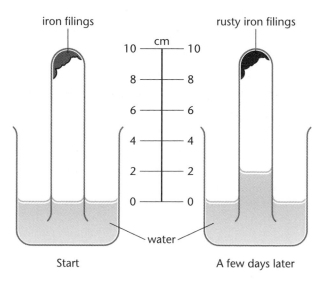

iron filings   rusty iron filings

Start   A few days later

The water very slowly rises and then stops where shown.
Rust is iron oxide.

3.4 Elements of Thar

Metals are good conductors of both heat and electricity.
Most non-metal elements are not.

No metal elements are gases at ordinary room temperature (20 °C).

The diagrams and table give you some information about some elements.
The names of the elements are those used by aliens on the planet Thar.

1 (a) Write down the Tharian names of three non-metal elements that you can see on the diagrams or in the table.
(b) Write down the English names of these elements alongside your answers.

2 (a) Write down the Tharian names of five metal elements.
(b) Write down the English names of these elements alongside your answers.

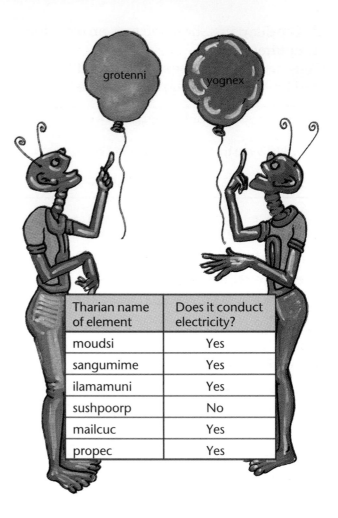

grotenni   yognex

Tharian name of element	Does it conduct electricity?
moudsi	Yes
sangumime	Yes
ilamamuni	Yes
sushpoorp	No
mailcuc	Yes
propec	Yes

3.5 Metals reacting with oxygen

Many metals will burn in air.

When a metal **burns** it **reacts** with oxygen. A new substance called a metal **oxide** is produced.

For example, magnesium burns to make a new substance called magnesium oxide. We can write down what happens in this chemical reaction as follows:

magnesium + oxygen → magnesium oxide

Some metals burn faster and brighter than others. We say that these metals are more **reactive** than the others.

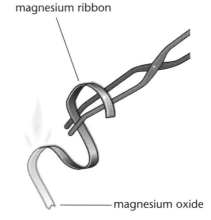

magnesium ribbon

magnesium oxide

1 Copy the sentences.
Fill in the blanks using the **bold** words.

Magnesium _____ very brightly in air.
It _____ with oxygen to make a new substance called magnesium _____.

Magnesium burns quickly and brightly.
This tells us that it is a _____ metal.

2 Look at the diagram.
Then copy and complete the following.

copper + _____ → _____ oxide

Copper does not burn brightly like _____.
This tells us that copper is a less _____ metal
than magnesium.

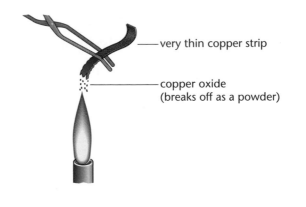

very thin copper strip

copper oxide
(breaks off as a powder)

• •

3.6 **Metals reacting with water**

Sodium reacts quickly with **water**.

Magnesium reacts much more slowly
with water.
It reacts faster if the water is in the
form of **steam**.

The faster a metal reacts with water
the more **reactive** we say that the
metal is.

Copper does not react with water at all.
It is an unreactive metal.

When metals react with water (or
steam) a gas called **hydrogen** is
produced.

1 Copy the grid below.
Write in the **bold** words that match the clues.
One of them has been done for you.

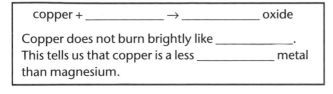

Across
3 Make up your own clue for this word.
6 A metal that does not react with water.
7 A metal that reacts slowly with water but more
quickly with steam.
Down
1 A gas produced when metals react with water.
2 You boil this to make steam.
4 Metals that react slowly with water will react much
faster with ____.
5 A very reactive metal.

2 The diagram shows a very small piece of
potassium reacting with water.

(a) What gas is produced by this reaction?
(b) The reaction is so fast that this gas
becomes very hot.
What then happens to the gas?
(c) The reaction produces another new
substance which dissolves in the water.
What is this new substance called?

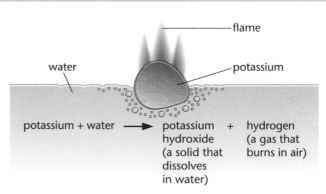

flame

water

potassium

potassium + water ⟶ potassium + hydrogen
hydroxide (a gas that
(a solid that burns in air)
dissolves
in water)

3.7 Which metals push hardest?

Some metals are more **reactive** than others.

For example, **iron** is a more reactive metal than **copper**. This means that iron can **push** copper out of a **solution** such as copper sulphate. The iron goes <u>into</u> the solution.

iron + copper sulphate → iron sulphate + copper
[solid]   [solution]   [solution]   [solid]

We say that the iron <u>displaces</u> the copper from the solution. So the reaction is called a **displacement** reaction.

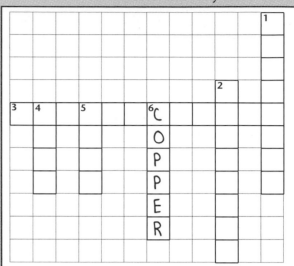

1 Copy the grid.
Write in the **bold** words that match the clues.
One of them has been done for you.

Across

3 One metal pushing another metal out of a solution is called a ____ reaction.

Down

1 A more reactive metal can push a less reactive metal out of a ____.

2 Copper is a less ____ metal than iron.

4 This metal is more reactive than copper.

5 'Displace' means the same as ____ out.

6 Make up your own clue for this word.

2 The top diagram shows what happens when you add zinc powder to copper sulphate solution.
Use information from the diagram to help you answer the following questions.

(a) What two changes do you see?

(b) What is the pink-brown powder that is produced?

(c) Copy and complete the sentences.

Zinc is a more _____ metal than copper. So the zinc _____ the copper from the copper sulphate solution.

(d) What is the colourless solution left in the tube at the end of the reaction?

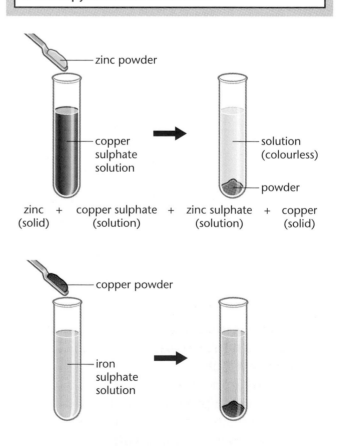

zinc   +   copper sulphate   +   zinc sulphate   +   copper
(solid)   (solution)   (solution)   (solid)

3 When you add some copper powder to some iron sulphate solution nothing happens. Why not?

Which metals react best?

Scientists often list metals in order of how reactive they are.

The **most** reactive metal is at the top and the **least** reactive metal is at the bottom.
This is called a **reactivity** series.

Sodium reacts quickly with cold water.
Zinc reacts <u>very</u> slowly with cold water and copper does not react at all.

You can use a reactivity series to <u>predict</u> how a metal will react before you actually try the reaction.

1 The box below shows the reactivity series for some metals.
(a) Copy the box.
Use the **bold** words to fill in the blanks.

_____ series	
_____ reactive	potassium
	sodium
	magnesium
	zinc
	copper
_____ reactive	silver

(b) Use the reactivity series to predict how fast (if at all) potassium, magnesium and silver will react with cold water.

2 (a) Magnesium ribbon burns brightly in air.
How brightly would you expect thin strips of the following metals to burn in air?
    (i) sodium
    (ii) zinc
(b) Hot copper powder reacts slowly with chlorine gas.
How quickly would you expect the following to react with chlorine?
    (i) hot silver powder
    (ii) hot zinc powder

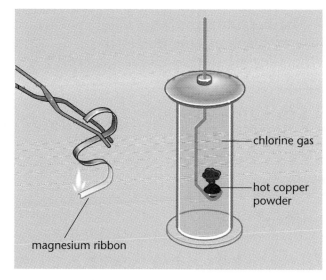

chlorine gas

hot copper powder

magnesium ribbon

magnesium powder   copper powder

3 (a) You have some zinc nitrate solution in two test tubes.
What would you expect to happen:
    (i) if you add some magnesium powder to one of the tubes?
    (ii) if you add some copper powder to one of the tubes?
(b) You should not try to displace zinc from zinc nitrate solution using sodium.
Why not?

zinc nitrate solution
(colourless)

- Zinc powder is grey.
- Magnesium nitrate solution is colourless.
- Copper nitrate solution is blue-green.

4.1 Chemical changes

Lots of changes happen in the world around us.

Some of these changes produce <u>new</u> <u>substances</u>. We say that these are **chemical** changes.

Examples of chemical changes are:
- burning,
- **metals** reacting with **acids**,
- your body **digesting** food and then using it for energy or to grow.

Changes that do <u>not</u> produce new substances are called **physical** changes.
Examples of physical changes are:
- sugar **dissolving**,
- water **evaporating**.

2 The diagram shows what happens when you put some calcium into water.
What two new substances are produced?

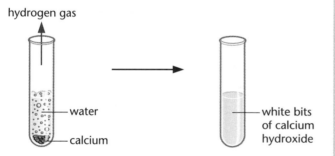

3 Copy the table. Then complete it.

Change	Chemical or physical?
cutting paper	
burning paper	
boiling water	
reacting calcium and water	

1 Copy the grid below.
Write in the **bold** words that match the clues. The word in the red box is also a bold word. Some of the letters of this word are already written in for you. So you may find it helpful to complete this word first.

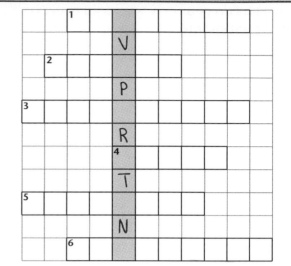

Clues

1 Changes that produce new substances.
2 and 4 A chemical change happens when these react with each other.
3 A physical change when you mix salt and water.
5 Changes that do not produce new substances.
6 A chemical change that happens to food.
Make up your own clue for the word in the red box.

- -

4.2 Acids

Many **fruits**, for example apples, oranges and lemons, taste 'tangy'.

They have a sharp and sour taste because they contain weak acids. Lemons, for example, contain citric **acid**.

Strong acids such as **hydrochloric** acid, **nitric** acid and **sulphuric** acid can damage your flesh and many other materials too.
We say that they are **corrosive**.

1 Copy the table.
Use the **bold** words to fill in the blanks.

Three strong acids are _____ acid _____ acid and _____ acid	Strong acids can harm you because they are _____
One weak _____ is citric acid	Weak acids taste tangy. They are contained in many _____

2 A car driver noticed that his battery was cracked. He removed the battery and replaced it with a new one.

The diagrams show what happened a few hours later.

(a) What happened to the man's hands and jumper?
(b) Why do you think this happened?
(c) What should the man have done to prevent these things happening:
    (i) when he was removing the damaged battery?
    (ii) after he had finished the job?

> You can make acid less corrosive by diluting it with plenty of water.

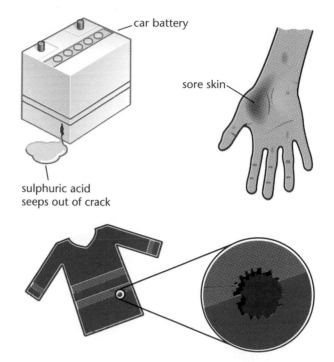

car battery

sore skin

sulphuric acid seeps out of crack

How can we tell whether something is an acid?

Litmus is a dye that can change colour.
In an **acid** litmus is red.
In an **alkali** litmus is blue.
Because it changes colour in this way we say that litmus is an <u>indicator</u>.

Water is neither an acid nor an alkali.
We say that water is **neutral**.
Litmus is purple in water.

Universal indicator can be many different colours. It tells you whether an acid or an alkali is **strong** or **weak**.

1 Copy the diagrams.
Add the missing labels using the **bold** words.

Litmus

what the colour indicates
_____ _____ _____

Universal indicator

pH
0 1 2 3 4 5 6 7 8 9 10 11 12 13 14

more _____   weak _____

←— acid —→ | ←— alkali —→

_____

2 Copy the table.
Fill in the second column by matching the following words with the pH numbers.

neutral   **strong acid**   **strong alkali**

weak acid   **weak alkali**

pH number	What it means
0–1	
5–6	
7	
8–9	
13–14	

4.4 Getting rid of an acid with an alkali

If you mix some **acid** with just the right amount of **alkali** they cancel each other out. You end up with a neutral solution.
We say that the acid and alkali **neutralise** each other.
A chemical reaction called <u>neutralisation</u> has happened.

Neutralisation reactions produce two new **substances** – a **salt** and **water**.

2 Luke puts some acid plus a few drops of universal indicator into a test tube.
Then he adds alkali one drop at a time.
The diagrams show what happens.

(a) Describe what happens to the colour of the solution.
(b) What do these changes in colour tell you?
(c) How many drops of alkali should Luke have added to get a neutral solution?

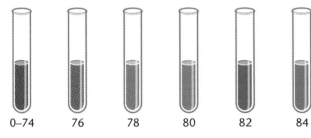

| 0–74 | 76 | 78 | 80 | 82 | 84 |

Number of drops of alkali added

1 Copy the grid below.
Write in the **bold** words that match the clues.
One of them has been done for you.

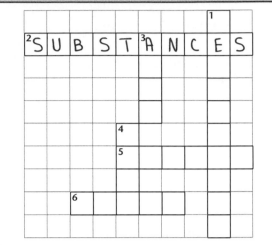

Across
2 Make up your own clue for this word.
5 You can neutralise an acid with this.
6 A new substance produced in a neutralisation reaction.

Down
1 When acids and alkalis react they ____ each other.
3 You can neutralise an alkali with this.
4 A new substance produced in a neutralisation reaction.

- - -

4.5 Using neutralisation reactions

Acids can cause problems.
- Your **stomach** makes acid to help you to digest food. But if it makes too much acid this can cause indigestion.
- Acid **rain** can kill the fish in lakes.
- **Bacteria** in your mouth can make acids that rot your teeth.

We can cure these problems by using alkalis to **neutralise** the **acids**.

We can also use substances called carbonates or bicarbonates to neutralise acids. These produce a gas called **carbon dioxide** when they react with acids.

1 Copy the grid below.
Write in the **bold** words that match the clues. If your answers are correct the word in the red box will also be a bold word.

Clues
1 These can produce acids that make your teeth decay.
2 This produces acid that sometimes gives you tummy-ache.
3 If this is acid it can harm fish in lakes.
4 This gas is made when you add acid to a carbonate.
5 You can use alkalis to ____ acids.
   Make up your own clue for the word in the red box.

2 The diagrams show one way of making fizzy lemonade.

(a) What two substances react to make the drink fizzy?

(b) Why does this reaction make the drink fizzy?

(c) The lemonade powder does <u>not</u> contain enough sodium bicarbonate to neutralise all of the citric acid.

What do you think is the reason for this?

dry lemonade powder (citric acid + sodium bicarbonate)

water

The two solids in lemonade powder dissolve and then react with each other.

● ●

4.6

How do metals react with acids?

Some metals, such as **magnesium**, react with **acid**.

Two new substances are produced in this reaction:

● a compound called a **salt**,

● a gas called **hydrogen**.

Salts are solid substances but many of them dissolve in water. This means that the reaction produces a <u>solution</u> of the salt.

Hydrogen gas burns with a slight '**pop**' when you light it.

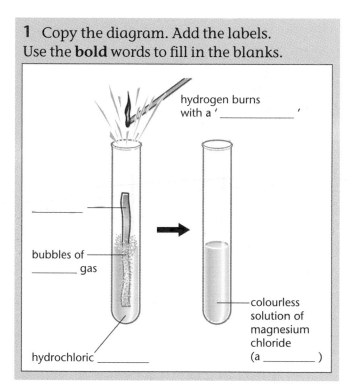

1 Copy the diagram. Add the labels. Use the **bold** words to fill in the blanks.

hydrogen burns with a '_____'

bubbles of _____ gas

hydrochloric _____

colourless solution of magnesium chloride (a _____)

2 Zinc reacts with hydrochloric acid in the same way as magnesium.

(a) You want to prove that the reaction produces hydrogen.

How would you do this?

(b) After the reaction is over you gently evaporate all the water.

What is the white solid left behind in the test tube?

hydrogen   steam

hydrochloric acid

zinc

4.7 Salt and salts

There are many different kinds of **salt**.
The kind that you put on your food is called common salt or **sodium chloride**.
It is a compound made from two elements:
● a metal called **sodium**,
● a non-metal called **chlorine**.

Other salts also contain a **metal** element joined to one (or more) **non-metal** elements.

2 All the crystals of a particular kind of salt are the same colour and shape.
For example, sodium chloride crystals are colourless cubes.

1 Copy the sentences.
Fill in the blanks using the **bold** words.

Another name for common salt is _____ _____.
Its name tells you that it contains two elements, _____ and _____.
Copper sulphate is also a _____. It contains: ● an element called copper which is a _____.   ● two elements called sulphur and oxygen, each of which is a _____.

| potassium chloride | copper sulphate | magnesium nitrate | calcium sulphate | silicon oxide (quartz) |

Look carefully at the diagrams of some crystals.
Then copy the table and fill in the last two columns using the following words:

colourless   blue

cube   diamond-shaped

needle   hexagonal (six-sided)

Name of crystal	Shape	Colour
potassium chloride		
copper sulphate		
magnesium nitrate		
calcium sulphate		
silicon oxide (quartz)		

4.8 Other kinds of chemical reaction

There are many different kinds of chemical reaction.

In some chemical reactions, a substance breaks down (decomposes) into two or more simpler substances.
These are called **decomposition** reactions.

In other chemical reactions, **oxygen** joins with another element.

This happens:
● when metals or fuels burn (burning is also called **combustion**),
● when you get energy from your food (this is called **respiration**),
● when iron rusts.
Combustion, respiration and rusting are all **oxidation** reactions.

1 Copy the table.
Fill in the blanks using the **bold** words.

_____ (burning)	These are all _____ reactions (another element joining with _____)
_____ (getting energy from food)	
rusting	
splitting a substance up into simpler parts	This is called a _____ reaction

2 The diagrams show what happens when you heat copper carbonate.

(a) What change can you <u>see</u> during this reaction?

(b) What <u>two</u> new substances are produced?

(c) What kind of reaction is this?
Give a reason for your answer.

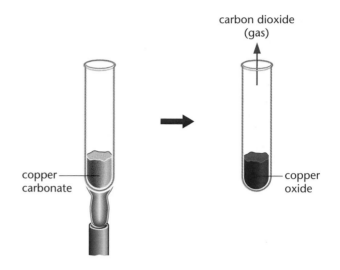

carbon dioxide (gas)

copper carbonate

copper oxide

4.9 Writing down chemical reactions

We often describe chemical reactions using <u>word equations</u>.

Here are two examples.

| hydrogen | + | oxygen | → | water |

tells you that

| hydrogen | <u>and</u> | oxygen | <u>react to make</u> | water |

| calcium carbonate | → | calcium oxide | + | carbon dioxide |

tells you that

| calcium carbonate | <u>splits up to make</u> | calcium oxide | <u>and</u> | carbon dioxide |

1 Write down the following word equation. Underneath it, write down what it tells you.

| sodium | + | chlorine | → | sodium chloride |

_____   _____   _____   _____   _____

2 Write down the following word equation. Underneath it, write down what it tells you.

| mercury oxide | → | mercury | + | oxygen |

_____   _____   _____   _____   _____

3 Ammonium chloride splits up when you heat it into ammonia and hydrogen chloride.
Write down the word equation for this reaction.

4 Potassium reacts with water to make potassium hydroxide and hydrogen.
Write down the word equation for this reaction.

5.1 Different types of rock

We call the <u>molten</u> rock under the Earth's crust **magma**.

When it sets it forms **igneous** rocks such as **basalt** and **granite**.

The Earth's **crust** is made up of hundreds of different kinds of <u>solid</u> rock. A few of them are shown in the key.

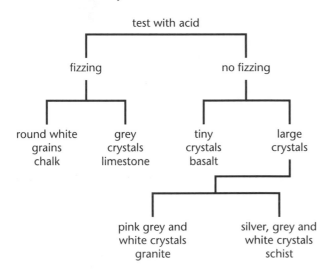

test with acid

fizzing — no fizzing

round white grains — chalk
grey crystals — limestone
tiny crystals — basalt
large crystals

pink grey and white crystals — granite
silver, grey and white crystals — schist

2 Look at the key.

(a) Use the key to name the rock in the drawing.

(b) Write down <u>three</u> features of chalk.

(c) Write down <u>one</u> difference between basalt and granite.

1 Copy the diagram below.
Write in the **bold** words that match the clues.
One has been done for you.

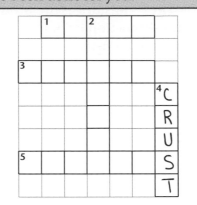

Across
1 Molten rock.
3 Made when magma sets quickly.
5 Rocks formed when magma sets.
Down
2 Made when magma sets inside the crust.
4 Make up your own word for this clue.

This rock does not fizz with acid.

5.2 Getting new rocks from old

We divide rocks into three main groups.

Rock type	Made	Examples
igneous	when **magma** cooled	granite, basalt
sedimentary	under the sea	limestone, sandstone
metamorphic	from other rocks by **heat** and pressure	marble (from limestone) slate (from mudstone)

1 Copy the grid.
Then write in the **bold** words to match the clues.
If your answers are correct, the word in the red box will also be a bold word.

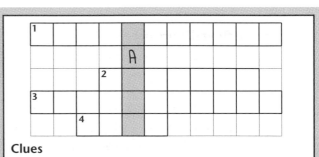

Clues
Volcanic rocks are …**2**… rocks.
We call rocks made from deposits in the sea …**3**… rocks.
Both of these can be changed by …**4**… and pressure into …**1**… rocks.
Make up your own clue for the word in the red box.

2 Sedimentary rocks are often made up of different-sized grains.

Different-sized grains take different lengths of time to settle in water.
Tim did an experiment to find out how quickly different-sized grains settled.

Grains	Size of grain (mm)	Time to settle (seconds)
gravel	over 2	1
sand	0.02 to 2	2
silt	0.002 to 0.02	240
clay	less than 0.002	still settling at end of lesson

(a) What do Tim's results show?
(b) Grains that settle slowly are carried further out to sea than grains that settle quickly.
Copy the diagram.
Choose from sand, silt and clay to complete the boxes.
Use Tim's results table to help you.

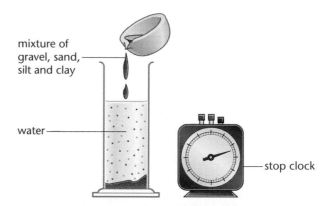

mixture of gravel, sand, silt and clay

water

stop clock

Tim shook the mixture. Then he left it to settle.

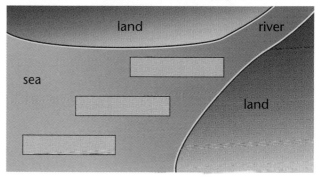

land

river

sea

land

Sediments in the sea near a river estuary.

5.3 The rock cycle

In nature, rocks are <u>recycled</u> in two ways:

$$\text{any rock} \xrightarrow{\text{melting}} \text{magma} \xrightarrow{\text{solidifying}} \textbf{igneous rock}$$

$$\text{any rock} \xrightarrow[\text{settling}]{\text{weathering}} \text{bits of rock} \xrightarrow{\text{transport and}} \textbf{sedimentary rock}$$

Rocks can also be <u>changed</u>.

$$\text{igneous or sedimentary rock} \xrightarrow[\text{pressure}]{\text{heat and}} \textbf{metamorphic rock}$$

1 Copy the flow diagram.
Write the correct **bold** words in the yellow boxes.

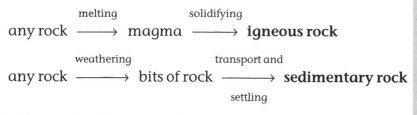

transport and settling

heat and pressure

bits of rock

weathering

heat and pressure

solidifying

melting

magma

2 Write a story about how a small grain from some granite on a mountain becomes part of some new sedimentary rock under the sea.

Include these words in your story:

weathering
river
sea bed
sediment
buried

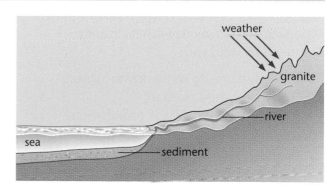

weather

granite

river

sea

sediment

5.4 How the weather breaks up rocks

Rocks are broken up by weathering.

Weathering process	What happens to the rocks
heating and cooling	they **expand** and **contract**, then they crack
water freezes in cracks	water expands as it **freezes**, so the cracks get bigger
sand is blown by **wind**	sand **wears** the rocks away

wind-blown sand

2 (a) The rock in the picture above is worn mainly at the base.
Why do you think this is?
(b) Which part of the cliff in the picture is the most worn?
What does this tell you about sandstone and shale?

1 Copy the grid below.
Write in the **bold** words that match the clues.
If your answers are correct, the word in the red box will also be a bold word.

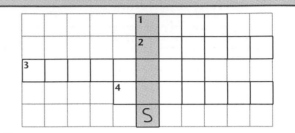

Clues
1 Moving air.
2 This word means get bigger.
3 This word means get smaller.
4 When water turns to ice it _____.
Make up your own clue for the word in the red box.

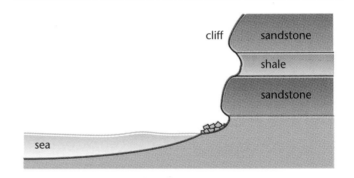

cliff
sandstone
shale
sandstone
sea

5.5 Acids in the air

These gases in the air dissolve in rain to make acids:
- **carbon dioxide** (a natural part of air)
- **sulphur dioxide** ⎫
- **nitrogen oxides** ⎭ pollutants

Acids make limestone fizz and dissolve.
We call this **chemical** weathering.
The more we pollute the air with these gases, the faster the weathering.

2 Their teacher gave Anita and Chris six rock samples. She asked them to design an experiment to find out which ones are damaged by acid rain.

Their first job was to write down lists of:
(a) the things they needed,
(b) how they would do the experiment, including how to make the test fair,
(c) safety precautions that they must take.
Write down your own lists for (a), (b) and (c).

1 (a) Copy the diagram. Then use the **bold** words to complete the boxes.

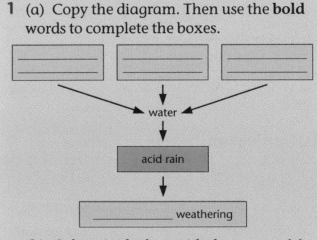

water

acid rain

_____ weathering

(b) Colour in the box with the name of the gas that is also found in clean air.

Things we can do with limestone

We quarry **limestone** for building stone.
We also use it to make useful chemicals.

$$\text{limestone} \xrightarrow{\text{heat}} \text{quicklime} \xrightarrow{\text{water}} \text{slaked lime}$$

Chemical	Common name
calcium carbonate	limestone
calcium oxide	**quick**lime
calcium hydroxide	slaked lime

We use **slaked** lime to make the lime-water
that we use to test for carbon **dioxide**.

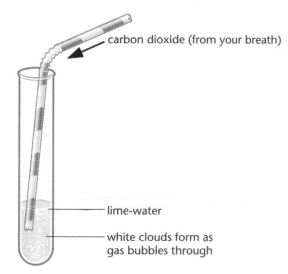

carbon dioxide (from your breath)

lime-water

white clouds form as
gas bubbles through

1 Copy the grid below.
Write in the **bold** words that match the clues.

Across
3 Lime used to make lime-water.
4 This lime is calcium oxide.
5 A rock made of calcium carbonate.
Down
1 Slaked lime is _____ hydroxide.
2 Lime-water is a test for carbon _____.

2 This is what happens when we use lime-
water to test for carbon dioxide.

lime-water + carbon dioxide → calcium carbonate (tiny white particles)

Look at the diagram. Carbon dioxide gas is
given off when the acid reacts with the
limestone.

Describe what you will
see as the chemical
reactions happen in:
(a) the flask,
(b) the boiling tube.

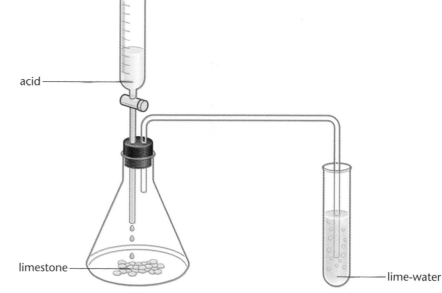

acid

limestone

lime-water

5.7 Getting metals from rocks

We find a few metals as pure (native) metals in rocks. We find most metals mixed with other substances in the rocks, as ores.

Metal	Found as
gold	**native** gold (the metal itself)
iron	ore (**haematite**)
sodium	ore (rock salt)
aluminium	**ore** (bauxite)

We get metals from their ores in different ways.

For example:
- we get iron by heating iron ore with coke and limestone in a **blast** furnace,
- we get aluminium from bauxite by **electrolysis**.

2 Look at the diagram.

(a) Write down the name of the iron compound in iron ore.

(b) In a blast furnace the oxygen from iron oxide joins with carbon to make waste carbon dioxide.

Where does the carbon come from?

(c) The temperature near the bottom of a blast furnace is 1200 °C.

What does this high temperature do to the iron that is produced in the furnace?

1 Copy the grid.
Write in the **bold** words that match the clues. If your answers are correct, the word in the red box will also be a bold word.

Clues
1 An ore of iron.
2 Bauxite is aluminium _____.
3 Furnace for getting metal from ore.
4 We find gold in this form.
5 A way of getting aluminium from ore.
   Make up your own clue for the word in the red box.

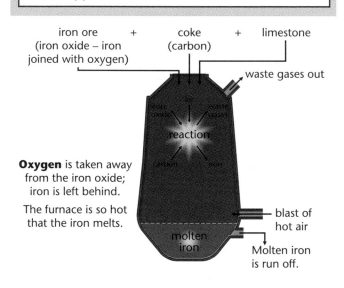

iron ore + coke + limestone
(iron oxide – iron
joined with oxygen)   (carbon)

waste gases out

Oxygen is taken away from the iron oxide; iron is left behind.

The furnace is so hot that the iron melts.

molten iron

blast of hot air

Molten iron is run off.

. . . .

5.8 A problem with metals

Metals react with substances from the air. They go dull and **corrode**.
For example iron **rusts** when air and water are present.

Metals corrode faster in **polluted** air than in clean air.
We can protect metals using a coating of:
- paint,
- **plastic**,
- oil,
- another metal (for example iron is coated in **tin** or zinc).

1 Copy the grid.
Write in the **bold** words that match the clues. If your answers are correct, the word in the red box will also be a bold word.

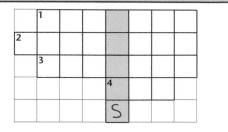

Clues
1 What metals do in air.
2 Air affects metals faster when it is _____.
3 and 4 Two coatings that protect iron.
   Make up your own clue for the word in the red box.

2 Look at the pictures.
Use your scientific knowledge to explain each of them.

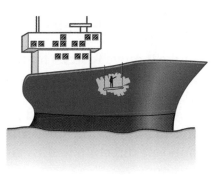

Steel is mainly iron.

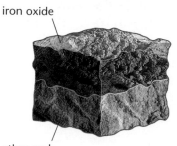

iron oxide

other rock

Iron ores never contain native iron.

Gardeners should clean and grease steel tools before they put them away for the winter.

Steel ships need to be painted at least once a year.

● ●

5.9

Why do we keep on polluting the air?

We burn **fuel** for the **energy** we need. When we burn fuels we also **pollute** the air with waste gases such as:
● nitrogen oxides,
● **sulphur** dioxide,
● carbon dioxide.

These dissolve in raindrops to make acid rain.

Air pollution harms:
● people's **health**,
● other animals,
● plants,
● buildings (corrodes stone),
● metals.

1 Copy and complete the sentences using the **bold** words.

> When we burn _____ , we _____ the air as well as getting _____.
> Pollution affects our _____.
> Nitrogen oxides and _____ dioxide are pollutants.

2 (a) Copy the diagram of the pH scale.

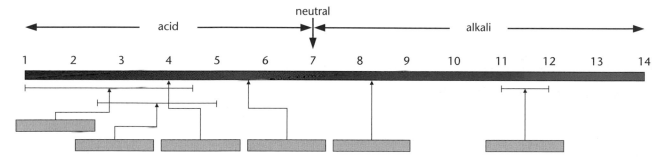

neutral

acid — neutral — alkali

1 2 3 4 5 6 7 8 9 10 11 12 13 14

Then add the information from the table.

(b) How can rain affect plants and animals in lakes? Use the idea of pH to explain your answer.

pH	Substance
4	lemon juice
2.5 to 5	acid rain
5.5	normal rain
8.2	sea-water
11–12	bleach
4.5 and below	water animals and plants die

1.1 How to make things move

If you apply a force to an object you can:

- make it **start** moving in the same direction as the force;
- make it move **faster** – for this to happen the force must be in the <u>same</u> direction as the object is moving;
- make it move **slower** and perhaps stop – for this to happen, the force must be in the <u>opposite</u> direction to the way the object is moving;
- make it move in a different **direction** – for this to happen the force must be <u>sideways on</u> to the movement.

1 Copy the diagrams and sentences. Use the **bold** words to fill in the blanks. The first one is done for you.

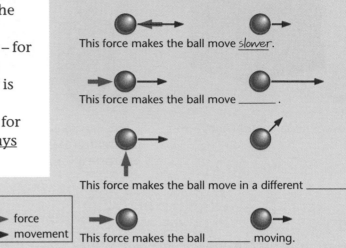

This force makes the ball move <u>slower</u>.

This force makes the ball move _____ .

This force makes the ball move in a different _____ .

Key
→ force
→ movement

This force makes the ball _____ moving.

2 Copy the table.
Add the missing arrows.

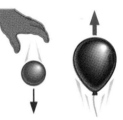

	Which way it moves	Direction of force
When you drop a ball	↓	
When you let go of a helium balloon		↑

1.2 Why do things slow down?

When an object slides along a **surface** in one direction, a **friction** force acts on it in the **opposite** direction. This force **slows** the object down.

When an object moves through the air in one direction, a friction force acts on it in the opposite direction.
This force slows the object down.
The force is called **air resistance** or **drag**.

1 Copy the grid.
Write in the **bold** words that match the clues.
One has been done for you.

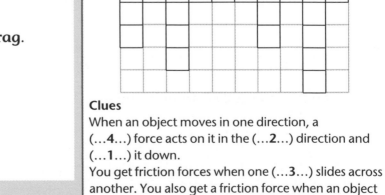

Clues
When an object moves in one direction, a (...**4**...) force acts on it in the (...**2**...) direction and (...**1**...) it down.
You get friction forces when one (...**3**...) slides across another. You also get a friction force when an object moves through the air. This is called air (...**6**...) or (...**5**...).

2 Look at the pictures.
Use them to help you to complete the
sentences.

> The table tennis ball slows down as it moves through
> the _____.
> This is because a friction force called _____
> acts on it.
>
> As the curling stone _____ from left to right
> across the ice, it gradually _____ down.
> This is because a _____ force acts on it in the
> _____ direction.

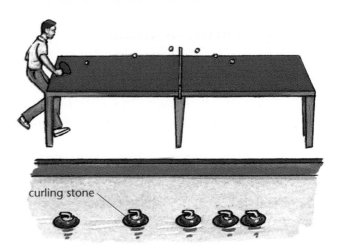

curling stone

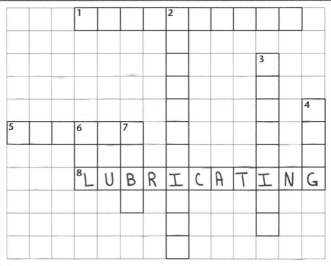

1.3 **How to reduce friction**

Cars and bicycles slow down unless
something keeps pushing them along all
the time.

This happens because of two forces:
- **friction** forces at the wheel **hubs**.
  You can reduce these by making the
  surfaces that slide across each other
  smooth and by **lubricating** them
  with **oil**.
- friction forces with the air – these are
  called air **resistance** or **drag**.
  You can reduce the air resistance of a
  car by making it more **streamlined**.

2 The diagrams show how Raj
investigated the drag force on some
model boats moving through water.

(a) Draw the shape of boat which moves
fastest through the water.
(b) Explain why this shape moves
fastest.
(c) Write down <u>four</u> things that Raj did
to make the tests fair.

1 Copy the grid below.
Write in the **bold** words that match the clues.
One has been done for you.

(crossword grid with answer at 8 across: L U B R I C A T I N G)

Across
1 Friction forces with the air are called air _____.
5 To reduce the friction between sliding surfaces you
must make sure they are very _____.
8 Make up your own clue for this word.
Down
2 To reduce drag, cars are _____.
3 Cars and bicycles are slowed down by _____
forces.
4 Another name for air resistance.
6 You use this to lubricate sliding surfaces.
7 In cars and bicycles, friction between sliding
surfaces occurs mainly at the _____.

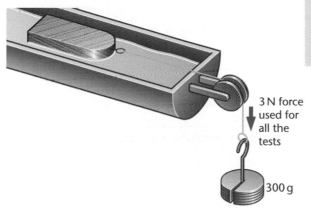

3 N force
used for
all the
tests

300 g

Shape of boat	(rectangle)	(rounded front)	(pointed front)
Time to travel 5 m	7 s	12 s	5 s

Boats are all the same mass
and made from the same
thickness of wood.

Making good use of friction

We use friction to slow things down.

For example:
- when you use the **brakes** on a car or bicycle you push friction pads against the moving wheels;
- a **parachute** gives you a lot of **drag** and makes you fall more slowly.

You also need plenty of friction between **surfaces**:
- so that your **soles** don't slip on the floor when you walk;
- so that tyres **grip** the road and don't **skid**.

1 Copy the table.
Use the **bold** words to fill in the blanks.

Example	Type of friction (surfaces or drag?)	Why friction is needed
tyres	_____	so they _____ the road and don't _____
_____	surfaces	so your feet don't slip when you walk
_____	_____	so you don't fall as fast
_____	_____	to slow down a car or bicycle

2 Look at the diagrams.
Use them to answer the following questions.

(a) The javelin is mostly smooth and has a very streamlined shape. Why is this?
(b) The part of the javelin that the athlete holds is rough. Explain why.
(c) The athlete rubs his hand in a powder called resin before throwing the javelin. Explain why, as fully as you can.

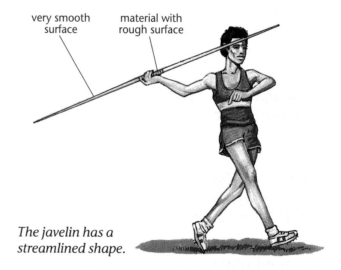

very smooth surface   material with rough surface

The javelin has a streamlined shape.

Balanced forces

Usually, there is more than one force acting on an object.

Sometimes these forces are **balanced**.
The object is then stopped (stationary) or it is moving in one direction at a steady speed.

Sometimes the forces acting on an object are <u>not</u> balanced.
An **unbalanced** force changes the speed of an object or makes it move in a different direction.

1 The table is about what a car does during a journey.

Copy the table and fill in the blanks using the **bold** words.

What the car does	Are the forces balanced or unbalanced?
slows down as it comes to red traffic lights	
waits for the traffic lights to go green	
travels round a roundabout at a steady speed	
speeds up to overtake a slow lorry	
travels along the motorway at a steady 60 miles an hour	

2 Lee drops a table tennis ball from the top of two flights of stairs.
The diagrams show what happens.

(a) What <u>two</u> forces act on the table tennis ball?

(b) What can you say about the size of these two forces:

(i) when the ball increases in speed during the first half of its fall?

(ii) when the ball falls at a steady speed during the second half of its fall?

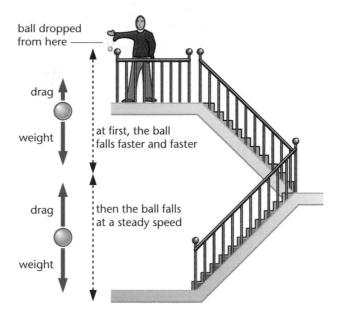

ball dropped from here

drag

weight

at first, the ball falls faster and faster

drag

weight

then the ball falls at a steady speed

● ●

1,6 How hard is it pressing?

Your **weight** is the **force** of gravity that **pulls** you towards the centre of the Earth.
Your weight **presses** down on whatever you are standing on.

To stop yourself sinking in soft ground you must **spread** your weight out over a large **area**. This then produces a smaller **pressure** on the ground.

If you want your weight to produce a larger pressure on the ground, you must make it press on a smaller area.

1 Copy the grid.
Write in the **bold** words that match the clues.
One has been done for you.
If your answers are correct, the word in the blue box will also be a bold word.

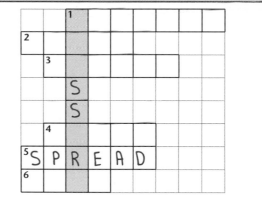

Grid shows: row with S, S; and row 5 spelling S P R E A D

Clues
Gravity (...**4**...) you towards the Earth.
This (...**2**...) is called your weight.
The weight of your body (...**1**...) against the ground.
To reduce this pressure you must (...**5**...) your weight over a larger (...**6**...).
You can produce a very large pressure by making your (...**3**...) act on a very small area.

2 Jenny used some squashy foam rubber to compare the pressure of some bricks.
The diagrams show what she did.

(a) Why is the foam more squashed in B than in A?

(b) How many bricks would you expect there to be in C?
Give a reason for your answer.

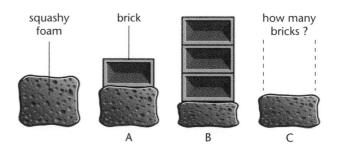

squashy foam   brick   how many bricks ?

A   B   C

1.7 Using forces to make things turn

Some things are fixed to the ground so they can't move to different places.
But they may still be able to **turn** around a **pivot** or axle.

Turning forces can act in opposite directions. They can make something turn **clockwise** or **anti-clockwise**.

Sometimes a clockwise turning force on an object is **balanced** by an anti-clockwise turning force. So the object does <u>not</u> turn.

> The hands of a clock go this way round.
>
>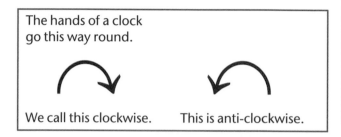
>
> We call this clockwise.   This is anti-clockwise.

1 Copy the diagram. Add the sentences. Fill in the blanks using the **bold** words.

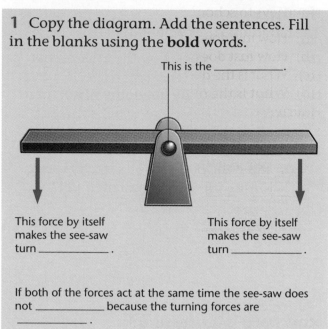

This is the _____.

This force by itself makes the see-saw turn _____ .

This force by itself makes the see-saw turn _____ .

If both of the forces act at the same time the see-saw does not _____ because the turning forces are _____ .

2 Look at the diagram.
Then copy and complete the sentences.

> To be able to see page 74 of this book you have to _____ page 73 _____ wise.
> As it turns, the page pivots around the _____ of the book.

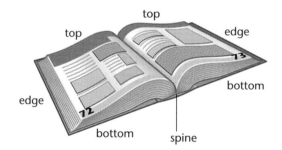

top

top   edge

edge   73

bottom

72

bottom   spine

1.8 How fast is it moving?

When something is moving fast, it travels a large distance in a short time.

We can calculate its speed like this:

$$\text{speed} = \frac{\textbf{distance}\text{ travelled}}{\textbf{time}\text{ taken}}$$

this line means 'divided by'

Example
A cyclist travels 100 metres in 5 seconds.

$$\text{speed} = \frac{\text{distance}}{\text{time}}$$

$$= \frac{100}{5}$$

$$= 20 \text{ metres per second}$$

On a journey you don't usually travel at the same speed all the time.
But you can still calculate your <u>average</u> speed.

1 Copy and complete the following using the **bold** words and then the numbers.

> <u>Calculating speed</u>
>
> An athlete runs 400 metres in 50 seconds.
>
> $$\text{speed} = \frac{\rule{2cm}{0.4pt}\text{ travelled}}{\rule{2cm}{0.4pt}\text{ taken}}$$
>
> = (replace the words by numbers)
>
> = (work out the answer) metres per second (m/s)

2 The table tells you about Emily's and Peter's journeys to school.

(a) How fast does Emily walk to the bus stop?
(b) How fast does Peter walk to school?
(c) What is the average speed of Emily's bus?
(d) What is the average speed of Emily's journey to school?

		Distance	Time
Emily	walk to bus stop	250 m	250 s
	wait for bus	—	300 s
	travel on bus	750 m	250 s
Peter	walk to school	800 m	1000 s

1.9 **Working out the pressure**

If you press with the <u>same</u> force on a <u>different</u> area you produce a different pressure.

Spreading the same force out over **double** the area will <u>halve</u> the pressure.

Making the same force act on an area ten times **smaller** will produce a pressure that is ten times <u>bigger</u>.

You can calculate pressure like this:

$$\text{pressure} = \frac{\text{force}}{\text{area}}$$

this line means 'divided by'

<u>Example</u>
Your hand has an area of 100 cm^2.
You push against a door with a force of 200 newtons.

$$\text{pressure} = \frac{\text{force}}{\text{area}}$$
$$= \frac{200}{100}$$
$$= 2 \text{ N/cm}^2 \text{ (newtons per square centimetre)}$$

2 A skier pushes down on his ski-ing stick with a force of 100 N.

(a) Calculate the pressure on the snow:
   (i) of the bottom of the stick,
   (ii) of the disc.
(b) Explain why the bottom of the stick has a fairly sharp end and then a disc a few centimetres higher up.

1 Copy the following.
Fill in the blanks using the **bold** words.

For the same force:
● if you make it act on half the area you will
   _____ the pressure;
● if spread the force out over ten times the area you will make the pressure ten times
   _____.

$$\text{pressure} = \frac{\quad\quad\quad}{\quad\quad\quad}$$

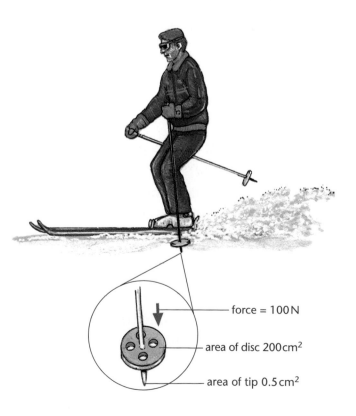

force = 100 N

area of disc 200 cm^2

area of tip 0.5 cm^2

2.1 How you see things

For you to be able to see an object, light must travel from the object into your **eyes**.

Most things do <u>not</u> give out their own light. They **reflect** light that has come from the Sun or from an electric light bulb.

Light travels in straight **lines** so it doesn't go round **corners**.
This is why you can't see round corners. It is also why you get a **shadow** whenever anything gets in the way of the light.

2 Look at the diagram.
Use the information on the diagram to explain each of the following.

(a) The flowers to the right of the wall have opened their petals.
(b) The flowers to the left of the wall haven't opened their petals.
(c) Arun can see the bird but not the cat.

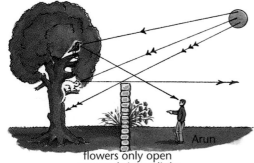

flowers only open
up petals in sunlight

1 Copy the grid below.
Write in the **bold** words that match the clues.
One has been done for you.

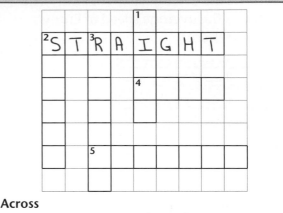

Across
2 Make up your own clue for this word.
4 You can only see things if light goes into your _____.
5 Light can't travel round _____.
Down
1 Light travels in straight _____.
2 If light can't get through an object you get a _____ behind it.
3 You can see most things because they _____ light.

2.2 Reflecting light

Some things, such as the Sun, electric light bulbs and TV sets give out their own light.

Most things <u>reflect</u> light that has come from something else. This page, for example, has a **bumpy** surface so it **reflects** light in **all** directions.

A **shiny** surface, such as a mirror, reflects a thin beam of light in only <u>one</u> direction.

A thin beam of light is called a **ray**.
A ray of light reflects from a mirror at the same **angle** as it strikes the mirror.

1 Copy the diagrams. Add the labels.
Fill in the blanks using the **bold** words.

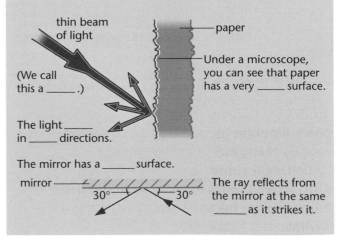

thin beam of light

paper

Under a microscope, you can see that paper has a very _____ surface.

(We call this a _____.)

The light _____ in _____ directions.

The mirror has a _____ surface.

mirror — 30° 30° — The ray reflects from the mirror at the same _____ as it strikes it.

2 Make a careful copy of the diagram.
Show on your diagram what happens next to
the ray of light.

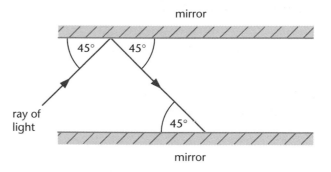

mirror

45° 45°

ray of
light

45°

mirror

● ●

2.3 ## Using mirrors

When a ray of light **strikes** a mirror at a
certain **angle**, it is **reflected** from the mirror
at exactly the **same** angle.

1 Copy the diagram. Add the labels.
Fill in the blanks using the **bold** words.

This ray of light
_____ the mirror
at an _____ of 70°.

70°

mirror

70°

The ray of light is
_____ from
the mirror at the
_____ angle.

2 Amy sends a ray of light towards a mirror.
She makes dots on a piece of paper to mark
the direction of the ray before it strikes the
mirror and after it is reflected.

She repeats the experiment four times using
different angles.
The second diagram shows her results.

(a) Copy the table.
Measure all of the angles for Amy's rays and
use them to fill in the table.

Angle that light strikes the mirror	Angle that light reflects from the mirror
10°	

(b) Amy must have marked one of the angles
wrongly. Which one was it?
(c) If you measured them carefully, the other
pairs of angles in the table aren't always
exactly the same.
Which is the more likely reason for this:
● Amy can't mark the rays exactly right?
● light isn't reflected at exactly the same
angle as it strikes the mirror?

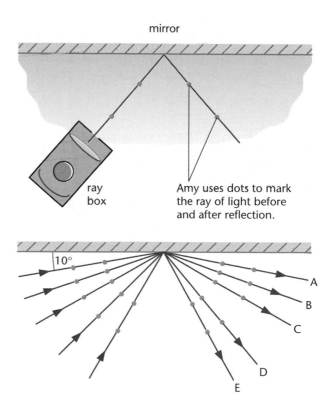

mirror

ray
box

Amy uses dots to mark
the ray of light before
and after reflection.

10°

A
B
C
D
E

2.4 Colours of the rainbow

White light, such as light from the Sun, is a mixture of many different colours. You can see these colours in a **rainbow**.

You can split white light up into a **spectrum** of colours using a **prism**.

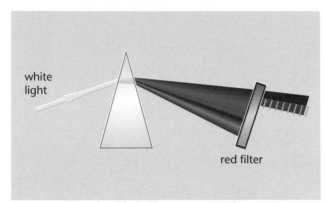

white light

red filter

You can use a **filter** to make white light coloured.
A **red** filter lets mainly red light through.
It **absorbs** other colours of light.

2 A filter is hidden inside a box.
The diagram shows what happens when you shine a beam of white light through a small hole in the box.

(a) What colour is the filter inside the box?
(b) What will happen:
 (i) if you shine blue light through the hole?
 (ii) if you shine red light through the hole?

1 Copy the grid below.
Write in the **bold** words that match the clues. One has been done for you.

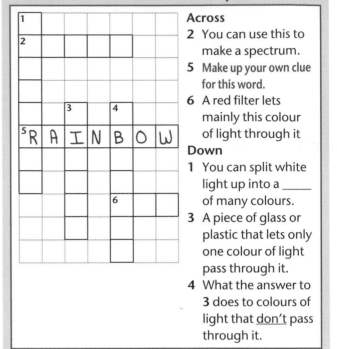

Across
2 You can use this to make a spectrum.
5 Make up your own clue for this word.
6 A red filter lets mainly this colour of light through it

Down
1 You can split white light up into a _____ of many colours.
3 A piece of glass or plastic that lets only one colour of light pass through it.
4 What the answer to **3** does to colours of light that <u>don't</u> pass through it.

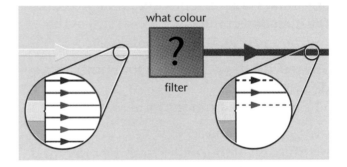

what colour

?

filter

2.5 Why do things look coloured?

You can see this page because it reflects light from the Sun (or from a light bulb).

The light that strikes the page is white.

The paper also looks **white** because it reflects most of **every** colour in the white light.

The print looks **black** because it **reflects** hardly any light of any colour.

Part of the page looks **blue** because it reflects blue light. The other colours in white light are **absorbed**.

1 Copy the diagram. Add the labels.
Fill in the blanks using the **bold** words.

In white light:

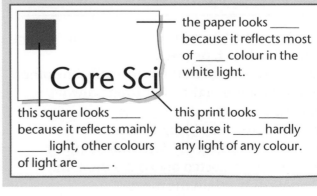

Core Sci

the paper looks _____ because it reflects most of _____ colour in the white light.

this square looks _____ because it reflects mainly _____ light, other colours of light are _____ .

this print looks _____ because it _____ hardly any light of any colour.

2 Look at the picture of a flowering plant. Then answer the following questions.

(a) Why do the leaves on the plant normally look green?

(b) Why do the flowers normally look red?

(c) What would the plant look like if you looked at it:

(i) through a red filter?

(ii) through a green filter?

2.6 Comparing light and sound

Light and sound are like each other in some ways but they are different in other ways.

Light and sound both travel through air. But:

● light travels a lot **faster** through air,

● light can also travel through empty **space** (a **vacuum**).

You see light with your **eyes**.
You hear sounds with your **ears**.

Light can be different <u>colours</u>.
One sound can be a higher note than another sound.
We say that the sounds have a different **pitch**.

1 Copy the grid below.
Write in the **bold** words that match the clues.
If your answers are correct, the word in the blue box will also be a bold word.

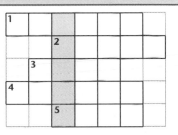

Clues

1 Light travels through air _____ than sound.

2 A high note has a different _____ than a low note.

3 You need these to hear with.

4 Another word for empty space.

5 You need these to see with.

Make up your own clue for the word in the blue box.

2 The picture shows a 100 metres race from many years ago.

Today, the starting signal sounds from the box behind each athlete.
This signal also starts a clock.
The clock records the time from the start to the finish for each athlete.

(a) Why is the new starting system fairer?

(b) Timekeepers used to start the stopwatch when they saw the puff of smoke from the starting pistol, not when they heard the bang. Why?

(c) 100 metres races used be timed to the nearest $\frac{1}{10}$ of a second. They are now timed to the nearest $\frac{1}{100}$ of a second. Why can races now be timed more accurately?

starting pistol

timekeeper with stopwatch

The error of starting and stopping a watch is often as much as $\frac{1}{10}$ second

2.7 **Making and hearing sounds**

To make a sound you must make something **vibrate**, for example a guitar string.

Vibrations will then travel through the air.

When these vibrations reach your ear they make your **eardrum** vibrate.

The vibrations pass through three **small bones** to your **inner ear**.

Your inner ear sends signals along nerves to your **brain**.

2 Workmen in a quarry use explosives, such as dynamite, to blast the rock.
The diagram shows three things that you can observe from a few miles away.

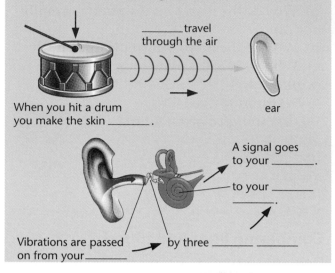

1 Copy the diagram. Add the labels.
Fill in the blanks using the **bold** words.

_____ travel
through the air

ear

When you hit a drum
you make the skin _____ .

A signal goes
to your _____ .

to your _____
_____ .

Vibrations are passed
on from your _____   by three _____ _____

(a) Write down the three things that you would observe in the right order.
Start with the thing that you would observe first.
(b) What does your answer to (a) tell you about how fast the three things travel?

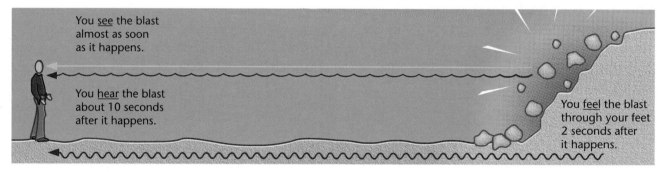

You see the blast
almost as soon
as it happens.

You hear the blast
about 10 seconds
after it happens.

You feel the blast
through your feet
2 seconds after
it happens.

2.8 **Different sounds**

Some sounds have a higher **pitch** than other sounds.
Sounds that have a high pitch are produced by things that vibrate quickly.

If something makes 500 to-and-fro vibrations each second we say that it has a **frequency** of 500 hertz (500 **Hz**).

Louder sounds are produced by larger vibrations. We say that these vibrations have a larger **amplitude**.

1 Copy the diagrams.
Write the sentences underneath.
Fill in the blanks using the **bold** words.

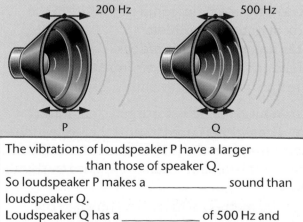

200 Hz

500 Hz

P

Q

The vibrations of loudspeaker P have a larger
_____ than those of speaker Q.
So loudspeaker P makes a _____ sound than
loudspeaker Q.
Loudspeaker Q has a _____ of 500 Hz and
loudspeaker P has a frequency of 200 _____.
Loudspeaker Q has a higher frequency so it makes a
sound with a higher _____.

2 The organ pipes shown in the diagram play notes with different frequencies.
But the notes sound similar to each other. All of these notes are called note A.

(a) The largest pipe makes a sound with a frequency of 55 Hz.
What does this tell you about the vibrations produced by the pipe?

(b) The smallest pipe shown on the diagram plays an A note that is one octave higher than the 220 Hz A note.
What is the frequency of the sound made by the smallest pipe?

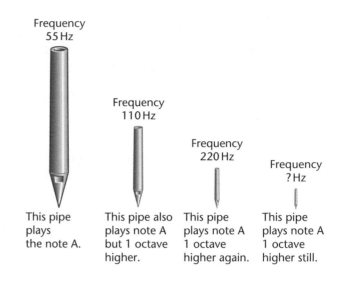

Frequency 55 Hz

Frequency 110 Hz

Frequency 220 Hz

Frequency ? Hz

This pipe plays the note A.

This pipe also plays note A but 1 octave higher.

This pipe plays note A 1 octave higher again.

This pipe plays note A 1 octave higher still.

2.9 How to bend light

A ray of light usually travels in a **straight line**.

But a ray of light can sometimes bend.
This can happen when the ray of light crosses the **boundary** from one material into another, for example from air into glass.
When light bends in this way we say that it is **refracted**.

1 Copy the diagram. Add the labels.
Fill in the blanks using the **bold** words.

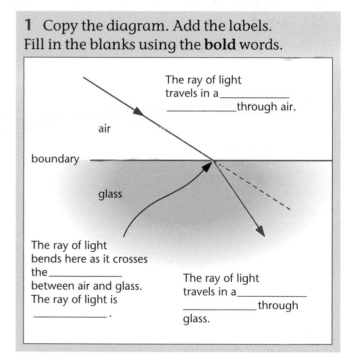

The ray of light travels in a _____ _____ through air.

air

boundary

glass

The ray of light bends here as it crosses the _____ between air and glass.
The ray of light is _____.

The ray of light travels in a _____ _____ through glass.

2 We sometimes want to say which way a ray of light is refracted.
It is easier to do this if we first draw a line at right angles (90°) to the boundary.

(a) What do we call a line at 90° to a boundary?

(b) Look at the diagrams. Then copy and complete the following sentences by choosing the correct blue word and filling in the blank.

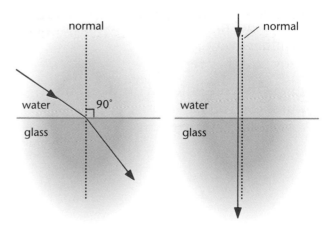

normal

water

glass

90°

normal

water

glass

When light passes from water into glass it is usually refracted away from/towards the normal.

But if the light is travelling along the normal it is not _____.

3.1 Making electricity by rubbing

If you **rub** two **different** materials together you can give them both an electric <u>charge</u>.

An object that is charged with **electricity** will attract other things, such as dust or bits of paper, towards it.

The electric charge on a charged object doesn't move anywhere but stays where it is. So we call it **static** electricity.

---

1 Make a copy of the grid below.
Write in the **bold** words that match the clues.

			¹D						
		2	U						
			³S						
4			T						

Clues

To produce an electric charge you need two (...**1**...) materials.

You then have to (...**2**...) these two materials together.

We call the charges that you produce in this way (...**3**...) (...**4**...).

Make up your own clue for the word in the blue box.

---

2 The diagrams show what can happen when you rub dust off a surface with a dry cloth.

(a) What happens to the glass surface straight after David wipes the dust off it?
(b) Why does this happen?

David wipes the dust off a glass table top.

The table top becomes covered with dust again straight away.

3.2 Two sorts of charges

There are two kinds of electric charge.
We call these charges:

positive (+) and **negative** (–).

Charges that are the same (**like** charges) push each other away.
We say that they **repel**.

Charges that are different (**unlike**) pull towards each other.
We say that they **attract**.

---

1 Copy the diagrams. Add the labels.
Fill in the blanks using the **bold** words.

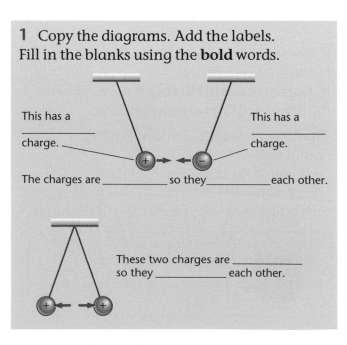

This has a
_____
charge.

This has a
_____
charge.

The charges are _____ so they _____ each other.

These two charges are _____ so they _____ each other.

2 The diagrams show the charges Malik produces when he rubs a balloon against his sweater.

Draw the right-hand diagram. Then copy and complete the sentences.

> When Malik rubs a balloon against his sweater:
> ● the balloon gets a _____ charge.
> ● the sweater gets a _____ charge.
> These charges are _____ so the balloon and the sweater _____ each other.

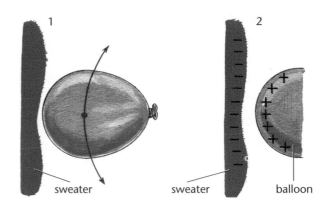

sweater   sweater   balloon

3.3 Electric currents

When electric charges **move** you get an electric current.

You can get a safe electric current from a **cell**. (Note: People often call this a **battery**, but you really need two or more cells to make a battery.)

To get a current, you must connect the two ends of a cell with things that an electric current can pass through.
We say that you must have a **complete** circuit of **conductors**.

To stop a current flowing round a circuit, you must **break** the circuit.
You usually do this using a **switch**.

1 Copy the diagrams. Add the labels. Fill in the blanks using the **bold** words.

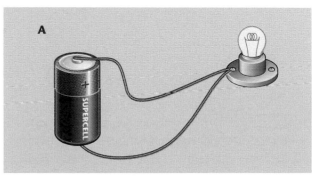

A current flows because there is a _____ circuit made from _____.

Electric charges _____ round the circuit.

This is a _____. Two or more of these make a _____.

This is a _____. You can use it to _____ the circuit and stop a current flowing.

2 The diagrams show three circuits.
The bulb does not light up in any of the circuits.
Explain, in each case, why the bulb doesn't light up.

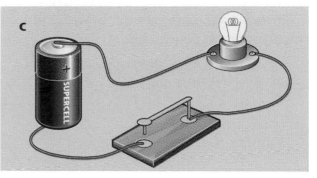

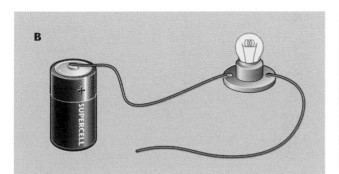

3.4 Other things that attract and repel

A magnet will attract anything that is made of **iron** or **steel**.
(Note: Things made from <u>stainless</u> steel may <u>not</u> be attracted by a magnet.)

When a magnet can move it will always turn round until:
- one end points **north** – this end of the magnet is called the north **pole**;
- the other end points **south** – this end of the magnet is called the south pole.

Two poles that are the same (**like** poles) push each other away.
We say that they **repel**.

Two poles that are different (**unlike**) pull towards each other.
We say that they attract.

1 Copy the grid below.
Write in the **bold** words that match the clues.
One has been done for you.

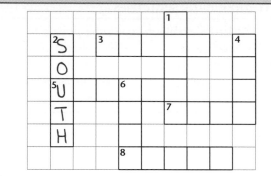

Across
3 A metal that is attracted by a magnet.
5 If two poles attract they must be _____.
7 If two poles repel they must be _____.
8 To repel a north pole you need a _____ pole.

Down
1 Two south poles _____ each other.
2 Make up your own clue for this word.
4 The end of a magnet that points north is called the north _____.
6 A metal that is attracted by a magnet.

2 Sara wants to use a bar magnet to find out which direction is north.

(a) Write down <u>three</u> ways that Sara can do this.
(b) What is the <u>same</u> about all three ways?

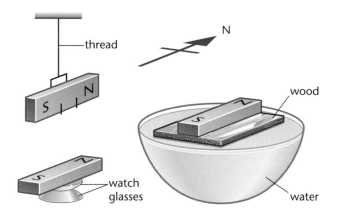

3.5 Magnetic fields

The area around a magnet where it pushes or pulls another magnet is called a magnetic **field**.

A **line** of magnetic **force** tells you which way the **north** pole of a magnetic **compass** will point if you put it on that line.

Lines of magnetic force also show you the shape of a magnetic field.

1 Copy the diagram. Add the labels.
Fill in the blanks using the **bold** words.

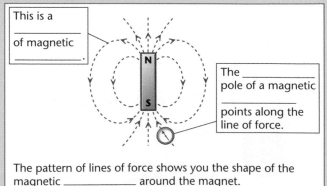

This is a _____ of magnetic _____.

The _____ pole of a magnetic _____ points along the line of force.

The pattern of lines of force shows you the shape of the magnetic _____ around the magnet.

2 The diagram shows you the lines of magnetic force between the north pole of one magnet and the south pole of another.

(a) Copy the diagram.
(b) Show which way the magnetic compasses at A, B and C will point.
(c) Add arrows to all the lines of magnetic force.

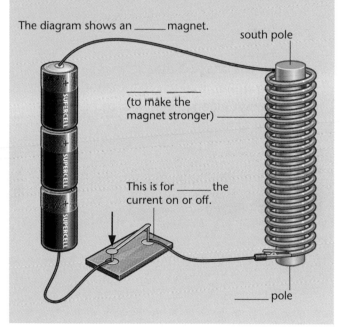

3.6 **Using an electric current to make a magnet**

When an electric current flows through a coil of wire, the coil acts like a bar magnet. One end of the coil is a **north** pole and the other end of the coil is a south pole. We call this an **electro**magnet.

You can make an electromagnet stronger by putting an **iron core** inside the coil.

You can turn an electromagnet off by **switching** off the current.

1 Copy the diagram. Add the labels. Fill in the blanks using the **bold** words.

The diagram shows an _____ magnet.

south pole

_____ _____ (to make the magnet stronger)

This is for _____ the current on or off.

_____ pole

2 Tom makes an electromagnet and then tests it with different cores inside the coil.

The diagrams show how many small nails the electromagnet picks up with each different core.

(a) What do Tom's results tell you?
(b) When Tom switches the current off, all the nails fall off except for one nail on the steel core.
Why do you think this nail doesn't fall off?

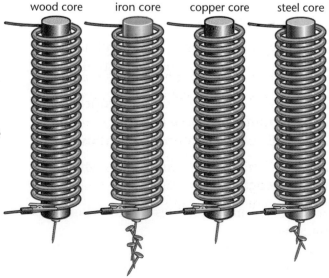

wood core   iron core   copper core   steel core

3.7 Building up circuits

You can use a **switch** to turn a bulb on and off.

For the switch to work, the current must go through the switch to get to the bulb (or to get back to the power supply).
We say that the switch and the bulb must be connected in **series**.

You can connect two bulbs in series with a power supply. The current flows through one bulb <u>and then</u> through the other bulb.

You can also connect two bulbs to a power supply so that the current flows through each bulb **separately**.
We then say that the bulbs are connected in **parallel**.

2 Look at circuits X, Y and Z.
Then write down, in each case, whether the bulbs are connected in series or in parallel.

1 Copy the diagram. Add the labels.
Fill in the blanks using the letters **A** and **B** and the **bold** words.

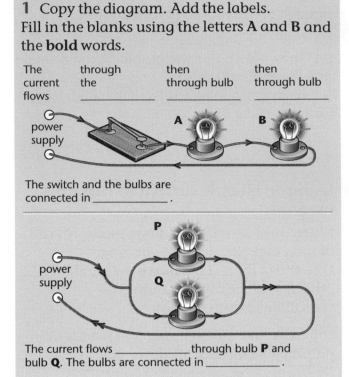

The   through   then   then
current   the   through bulb   through bulb
flows   _____   _____   _____

The switch and the bulbs are connected in _____ .

The current flows _____ through bulb **P** and bulb **Q**. The bulbs are connected in _____ .

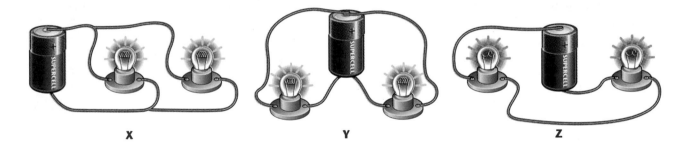

X   Y   Z

3.8 Using series and parallel circuits

The picture shows a circuit with a **cell**, a **switch** and a **bulb**.

When you draw a circuit, you don't need to draw a <u>picture</u> of what the circuit really looks like.
Instead, you can draw a circuit **diagram** using **symbols**.
Circuit diagrams are very easy to draw.

In a series circuit, it doesn't matter where you put the switch.

In a parallel circuit, it <u>does</u> matter where you put a switch.
A switch may turn off <u>all</u> of the circuit or it may turn off only <u>part</u> of the circuit.
It all depends on where the switch is.

1 Copy the diagram. Add the labels.
Fill in the blanks using the **bold** words.

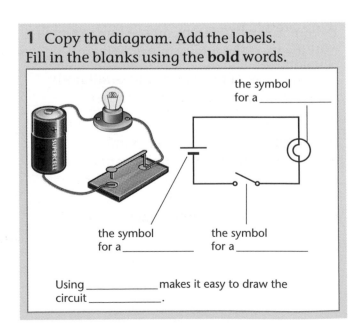

the symbol for a _____

the symbol for a _____

the symbol for a _____

Using _____ makes it easy to draw the circuit _____ .

2 Look at the diagram.
Then copy and complete the table.

Switch	Which bulbs it turns on and off
1	
2	
3	

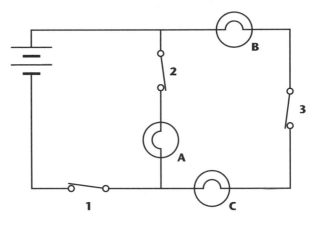

● ●

3.9 **Using electromagnets**

An electromagnet is very useful because you can switch it on and off.

You can use an electromagnet to make an electrically operated switch.
This is called a <u>relay</u>.

1 Paul and Hannah designed their own relay for switching a powerful motor on and off.
The diagram shows what their relay looked like.

(a) At first the relay didn't work.
When they pressed the switch, the steel bolt didn't move down far enough to touch the contacts.
So it didn't switch the motor on.
Suggest <u>four</u> different things that Paul and Hannah could do to solve this problem.
(b) When the relay was working properly, Paul pressed the switch and the powerful motor started up.
Explain, step by step, how this happened.
(c) When Paul stopped pressing the switch, the powerful motor stopped.
Explain, step by step, how this happened.
(d) Copy and complete the sentence.

With a relay you can turn on a _____ current by switching on a _____ current.

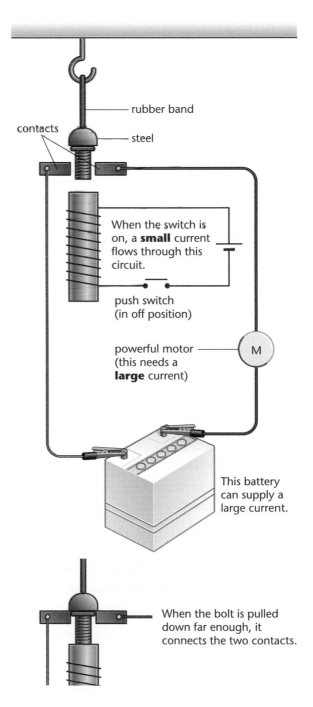

rubber band

contacts

steel

When the switch is on, a **small** current flows through this circuit.

push switch
(in off position)

powerful motor
(this needs a
large current)

M

This battery
can supply a
large current.

When the bolt is pulled down far enough, it connects the two contacts.

4.1 Switch on for energy

To make a light bulb work we must transfer **energy** to it by **electricity**.

The bulb then transfers energy to the surroundings as **light**.

Other electrical appliances transfer energy in different ways:

- a mixer transfers energy as **movement**;
- a radio transfers energy as **sound**;
- a kettle transfers **thermal** energy to the water inside it. (In other words, it makes the water **hot**.)

1 Copy the grid below.
Write in the **bold** words that match the clues.
One has been done for you.

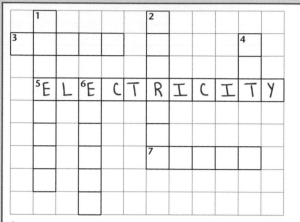

Across

3 A radio transfers energy as ____.
5 Make up your own clue for this word.
7 When you switch on a light bulb it transfers energy as ____.

Down

1 A mixer transfers energy as ____.
2 When something is hotter it has more ____ energy.
4 You use a kettle to make water ____.
6 We use electricity to transfer ____ to electrical appliances.

2 Copy the following sentences.
Complete them using information from the picture.

> We supply energy to a TV set by _____.
> We want the TV set to transfer energy as _____ and _____.
> The TV set also transfers _____ energy to its surroundings.

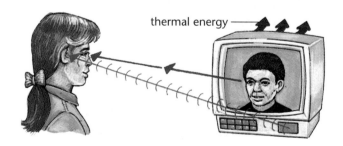

thermal energy

4.2 Energy from fuels

We can heat rooms, or cook food, by burning a **fuel** such as coal or gas.

When the fuel burns, it reacts with **oxygen** from the air.
So a fuel + oxygen is an energy **store**. This stored energy is called **chemical** energy.

When a fuel burns, the stored chemical energy is transferred as **thermal** energy.

1 Copy the flow diagram.
Use the **bold** words to fill in the blanks.

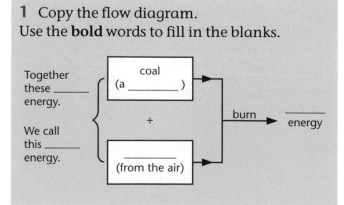

Together these _____ energy.

coal
(a _____)

We call this _____ energy.

_____ (from the air)

+

burn → _____ energy

2 When fuels burn they don't just transfer thermal energy to the surroundings. Energy is also transferred in other ways.

Copy the table.
Use the pictures to help you to complete it.

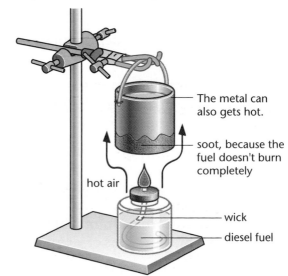

	We burn fuel because we want it to transfer energy as …
paraffin lamp	
motor cycle	

4.3 Using fuels to make electricity

In a power station, each large **generator** produces **electricity** as it spins.

The energy needed to make the generators spin usually comes from burning a **fuel**.

The thermal energy transferred by the burning fuel heats up **water** and turns it into **steam**.
The steam drives a **turbine** and the turbine drives the generator.

1 Copy the diagram.
Add the labels using the **bold** words.

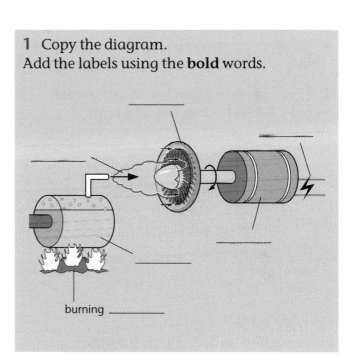

burning _____

2 Winston wants to find out how much energy is transferred by one gram of diesel fuel when it burns.
The diagram shows what he did and what happened.

(a) How much did the temperature of the water rise?
(b) How much energy was transferred to the water by burning 1 gram of diesel fuel?
(c) When 1 gram of diesel fuel burns in a diesel engine, more than 40 kJ of energy are transferred.
Why do you think Winston transferred a lot less energy than this to the water? Write down three reasons.

It takes 1 kilojoule (1 kJ) of energy to heat up the water in the can by 1 °C.

The metal can also gets hot.

soot, because the fuel doesn't burn completely

hot air

wick

diesel fuel

Winston found that 1 gram of the fuel heated up the water from 20 °C to 40 °C.

4.4 Some other ways of generating electricity

Many different energy sources can be used to generate electricity.

Power stations often use fuels as their energy **source**.

You can also generate electricity using:
- **wind**;
- **waves**;
- hot rocks deep in the Earth's crust – this is called **geothermal energy**;
- rain water trapped behind dams – we say that this water stores **potential** energy – this is transferred when the water flows downhill;
- sea-water trapped behind a barrage at **high tide**.

2 Electricity that is generated using water trapped behind a dam is called hydro-electricity.

Dams are very expensive to build.

You don't have to pay for the rain that collects behind the dam.

You can generate electricity whenever you need it.

Farmland and homes are flooded when you build a dam.

Copy the table.
Fill it in using the information on the diagram.

1 Copy the grid below.
Write in the **bold** words that match the clues.
One has been done for you.
If your answers are correct the word in the blue box will also be a bold word.

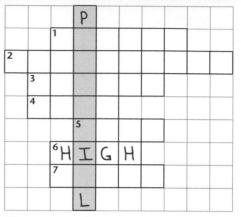

Clues
To generate electricity you need an energy (...**1**...).
If this energy comes from hot rocks it is called (...**2**...) (...**3**...).
You sometimes see large turbines on hill tops. These are driven by energy from the (...**4**...).
A barrage across a river estuary can trap sea-water when the (...**5**...) is (...**6**...).
(...**7**...) on the sea are another energy source.
Make up your own clue for the word in the blue box.

HYDRO-ELECTRICITY	
Advantages	Disadvantages

4.5 Thank you, Sun!

Most of our energy sources depend in some way on the **Sun**.

- We can transfer energy from the Sun's rays:
  - as thermal energy using solar **panels**,
  - as electricity using solar **cells**.

- **Plants** store energy from the Sun as they grow.
  We can use the plants as fuel, for example **wood** from trees.
  Coal and **oil** are formed from plants and animals that died millions of years ago.

- **Wind**, **waves** and **water** trapped behind dams all depend on the weather.
  Energy from the Sun causes the weather.

1 Copy the flow diagram.
Fill in the blanks using the **bold** words.

energy from the

used directly → solar _____ and solar _____

makes _____ grow → _____ (from trees)

millions of years → _____ and _____

causes weather → _____ (trapped by dams) _____ _____

2 Ali has just bought a tiny pocket radio that uses a solar cell to charge the battery inside it.

Ali tests his radio several times by charging up the battery for a while and then seeing how long the radio plays.
The table shows what happens.

What do Ali's results tell you?

solar cell

How long radio plays	Battery charged for 1 hour	Battery charged for 4 hours
bright sunlight	10 minutes	45 minutes
cloudy	2 minutes	9 minutes

4.6 Will our energy sources last forever?

Some energy sources, such as **coal**, **oil** and natural **gas**, took millions of years to form. We now use them so fast that they will run out before long.
We say that these energy sources are <u>non-renewable</u>.

We make **petrol** and **diesel** fuel from oil. So these fuels are also non-renewable. **Wood** comes from trees so it is a renewable source.

Other energy sources are being replaced all the time.
For example:
● the **wind** will keep blowing and will make **waves** on the sea for as long as the Sun keeps on shining;
● there will be **tides** for as long as the Earth keeps on spinning.
We say that these energy sources are <u>renewable</u>.

2 (a) Does hydro-electricity use a renewable or a non-renewable energy source?
Explain your answer as fully as you can.

(b) Where does the energy for hydro-electricity originally come from if you trace it back far enough?

1 The words in the table have their letters muddled up.
Sort out each group of letters to make the names of the energy sources given in **bold**. Then copy the table.

Renewable	Non-renewable
sewav	ilo
diwn	lopret
odwo	loca
setid	lidsee
	ags

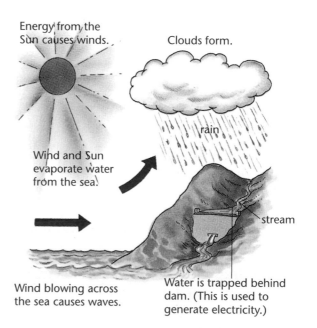

Energy from the Sun causes winds.

Clouds form.

rain

Wind and Sun evaporate water from the sea.

Wind blowing across the sea causes waves.

Water is trapped behind dam. (This is used to generate electricity.)

stream

4.7 Energy for your body

Your body needs a constant supply of energy.
You get this from your food (together with the oxygen you breathe).

The energy in food comes mainly from **carbohydrate** and **fat**.
Foods such as **rice**, bread and potatoes contain a lot of carbohydrate.
Foods such as butter, margarine and cooking **oil** contain a lot of fat.

Carbohydrates and fats store a lot of **chemical** energy.

Your body transfers energy from food:
- to keep you warm (**thermal** energy),
- when you move (**kinetic** energy),
- when you lift things up (to give them more **potential** energy).

2 Chris compared the energy in different foods by burning them.

(a) The diagrams show two things that Chris measured in each test. What other measurements does Chris need to make?
(b) Chris doesn't put the beaker over the food until after he has taken the Bunsen burner away. Explain why.
(c) How will Chris be able to tell which food stores most energy per gram?

1 Copy the grid.
Write in the **bold** words that match the clues.
The one in the blue box has been done for you.

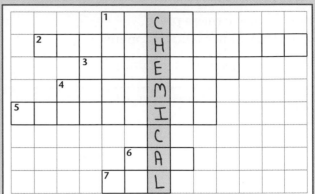

Clues
1 A food that is mostly carbohydrate.
2 One type of food that stores a lot of energy.
3 When you move your body has ____ energy.
4 To keep warm you need ____ energy.
5 When you climb stairs you give your body more ____ energy.
6 Another type of food that stores a lot of energy.
7 A liquid fat.
   Make up your own clue for the word in the blue box.

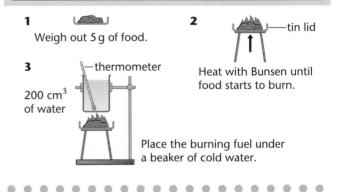

1 Weigh out 5 g of food.
2 tin lid — Heat with Bunsen until food starts to burn.
3 thermometer
200 cm³ of water
Place the burning fuel under a beaker of cold water.

4.8 Ways of storing energy

Some things, such as **food** and fuels, store energy in the chemicals that they are made from.
So this stored energy is called **chemical** energy.

Things that are lifted above the ground, for example the weights in a grandfather clock, also store energy.
We lift things up against the force of gravity so the stored energy is called **gravitational potential** energy.

Springy things that are stretched, or bent, or squashed, or twisted store energy.
Another word for springy is elastic.
So this kind of stored energy is called **elastic potential** energy.

1 Copy the information below.
Fill in the blanks using the **bold** words.

Energy can be stored:
- as _____ energy
  for example in fuels or in _____.

or

- as _____ energy.
  This can be either _____ (stored in springy things),
  or it can be _____ (stored in lifted up things).

2 Copy the table.
Use the the pictures to help you to fill in the blanks.

	Type of stored energy
toy car	_____
charged-up battery	_____
biscuits on high shelf	_____
	+ _____

A chemical reaction happens inside a battery when you recharge it

wound-up spring

4.9 **You don't only get what you want**

When energy is transferred, none of it is ever lost.
But not all of it is transferred in the way we would like it to be.

For example, for each **100** joules of energy transferred to a fluorescent strip light by **electricity**:

● about **30** joules are transferred from the tube as **light**;
● the other **70** joules of energy are transferred in other ways, mainly as **thermal** energy.

2 The diagram shows the energy transferred to and from an electric drill.

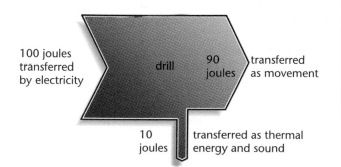

100 joules transferred by electricity

drill

90 joules transferred as movement

10 joules transferred as thermal energy and sound

(a) Write down, <u>in words</u>, what the diagram tells you.
(b) Which wastes least energy, the fluorescent tube or the drill?

1 Copy the diagrams. Add the labels.
Use the **bold** words and numbers to fill in the blanks.

100 joules of energy supplied by _____

fluorescent tube

30 joules of energy transferred as _____

70 joules of energy transferred as _____ energy

_____ joules supplied by electricity

fluorescent tube

_____ joules transferred as light

_____ joules transferred as thermal energy

5.1

The Sun and the stars

It <u>seems</u> as if the Sun **rises** each morning, moves across the sky and **sets** each evening. The **stars** <u>seem</u> to trace out circles across the night sky.

In fact, it is <u>not</u> the Sun and stars that move but the Earth.
The Earth **spins** round once every 24 **hours** or, in other words, once every day.

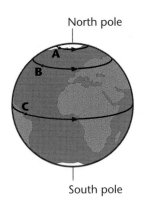

North pole

A is in the Artic
B is in the UK
C is on the equator

The arrows show how far A, B and C have moved in 2 hours.

South pole

1 Copy the diagram. Add the sentences. Fill in the blanks using the **bold** words.

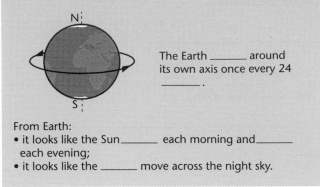

The Earth _____ around its own axis once every 24 _____ .

From Earth:
• it looks like the Sun _____ each morning and _____ each evening;
• it looks like the _____ move across the night sky.

2 The diagram shows three people, A, B and C, at different places on the Earth.

As the Earth spins:
(a) who is moving fastest?
(b) who is moving slowest?
(c) what happens to a person at the Earth's North or South pole?

- -

5.2

Why are the days longer in summer?

In summer in the UK:
• there are more hours of **daylight**;
• there are fewer hours of **darkness** than in winter.
The Sun also rises **higher** in the sky.

More **energy** reaches us from the Sun in summer. So it is **warmer** than in winter.

We get summer and winter in the UK because the Earth's axis is **tilted**.
In our summer, our northern half of the Earth is tilted **towards** the Sun.
In winter, our half of the Earth is tilted <u>away</u> from the Sun.

The Earth takes a **year** (just over 365 days) to go round the Sun. So we get a summer and a winter once each year.

1 Copy the grid below.
Write in the **bold** words that match the clues.
The one in the blue box has been done for you.

			¹D						
		2	A						
			³Y						
			L						
		4	I						
5			G						
	6		H						
			⁷T						

Clues

1 In winter there are more hours of _____ than in summer.
2 The weather in summer is _____ than in winter.
3 It takes a _____ for the Earth to go round the Sun.
4 We get summers and winters because the Earth's axis is _____.
5 Summers are warmer because we are getting more _____ from the Sun.
6 During the summer the Sun rises _____ in the sky.
7 During our Summer the northern part of the Earth is tilted _____ the Sun.

Make up your own clue for the word in the blue box.

2 Look at the diagram.
Then answer the questions below.

(a) What is special about March 21st and
September 23rd?
(b) What can you say about the hours of daylight
and darkness everywhere on Earth on March 21st
and September 23rd?

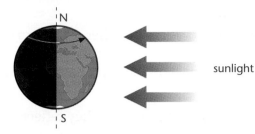

*On March 21st and September 23rd <u>no</u> part of the
Earth is tilted towards or away from the Sun.*

5.3 Stars and planets

We can see stars because they **give
out their own light**.
The Sun is a star. It is much nearer
to Earth than any other stars.

Whenever we look at stars in the
night sky they stay in the same
patterns.
These patterns of stars are called
constellations.

Planets look just like stars, but
they move very slowly through the
constellations. This happens
because the planets go round the
Sun just like the Earth does.

Planets don't give out their own
light. We can see them because
they **reflect** light that comes from
the Sun.

1 Copy the diagram. Add the labels.
Fill in the blanks using the **bold** words.

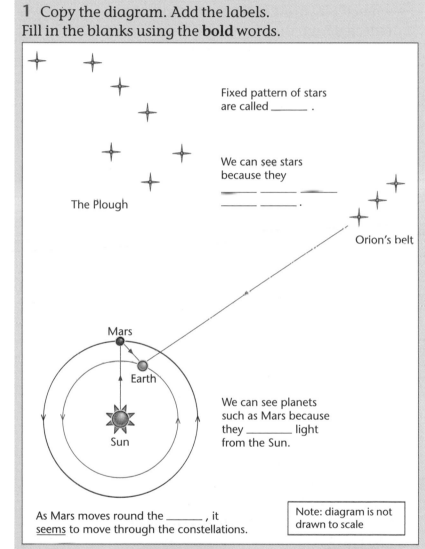

Fixed pattern of stars
are called _____ .

We can see stars
because they
____ ____ ____
____ ____ .

The Plough

Orion's belt

We can see planets
such as Mars because
they _____ light
from the Sun.

Mars

Earth

Sun

As Mars moves round the _____ , it
<u>seems</u> to move through the constellations.

Note: diagram is not
drawn to scale

2 As Earth and Mars move round their orbits, they
are sometimes on the same side of the Sun. At other
times they are on opposite sides of the Sun.

An astronomer on Earth looks at Mars through a
telescope. The pictures show what Mars looks like at
two different times.
(a) What is the main difference between the two
pictures?
(b) Suggest a reason for this difference.

One January

The next October

Mars through a telescope.

5.4 The solar system

The Earth and all of the other planets orbit the Sun.
We call the Sun and all its planets the <u>solar system</u>.

We can see planets because they reflect light that comes from the Sun.

A planet looks brighter and is easier to see:
- if it is large – a large planet reflects more of the Sun's light than a smaller one;
- when it is nearest to Earth – the light that is reflected from the planet hasn't spread out so much by the time it reaches Earth.

1 You can sometimes use little tricks to help you remember things.
For example you can remember the order of these musical notes:

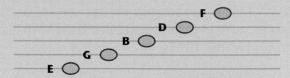

by remembering this sentence:

Every Good Boy Deserves Food

Make up your own way of remembering the order of the planets:

Mercury	nearest to Sun
Venus	
Earth	
Mars	
Jupiter	
Saturn	
Uranus	
Neptune	
Pluto	furthest from Sun

2 (a) (i) Which planets, besides the Earth itself, have humans known about for a very long time?
   (ii) Why have humans known about these planets for so long?
(b) (i) Which planets have been discovered fairly recently by looking through powerful telescopes?
   (ii) Why are these planets quite difficult to see even through a telescope?

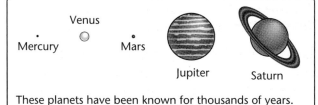

These planets have been known for thousands of years. They can be seen by the naked eye (without a telescope).

Uranus was first seen in 1781.
Neptune was first seen in 1846.
Pluto was first seen in 1930.

- -

5.5 Moons

The Moon moves in an **orbit** around the Earth. So we say that the Moon is a **satellite** of the Earth.

We can see the Moon because it **reflects** light that comes from the Sun.

The Moon sometimes goes into the Earth's **shadow**.
When this happens we cannot see the Moon. We say that there is an **eclipse** of the Moon.

1 Copy the diagram. Add the labels.
Fill in the blanks using the **bold** words.

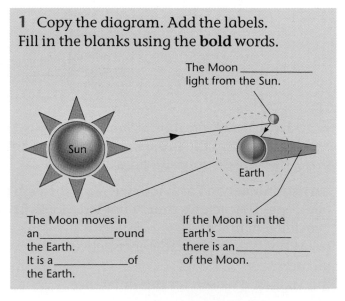

The Moon _____ light from the Sun.

The Moon moves in an _____ round the Earth.
It is a _____ of the Earth.

If the Moon is in the Earth's _____ there is an _____ of the Moon.

2 (a) Measure the diameter of balls A, B and C on the diagram.
Then write down your measurements:
diameter of ball A =   mm
diameter of ball B =   mm
diameter of ball C =   mm

(b) How many times bigger in diameter:
(i) is ball B than ball A?
(ii) is ball C than ball A?

(c) How many times further away from X:
(i) is ball B than ball A?
(ii) is ball C than ball A?

(d) Compare your answers to (b) and (c). What does this tell you?

(e) From Earth, the Sun and the Moon look almost exactly the same size. Explain why.

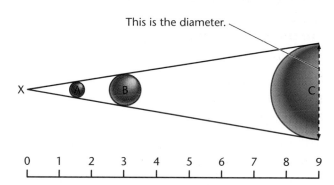

This is the diameter.

Balls A, B and C all <u>look</u> the same size to a person at X.

Artificial satellites

5.6

The Moon is the Earth's **natural** satellite.

Humans have also put a lot of **artificial satellites** into **orbit** around the Earth.

Astronomers can see stars more clearly from satellites. This is because the satellites are above the Earth's **atmosphere**.

You can also look down from a satellite and observe the world's **weather**.

2 The diagram shows a weather observation satellite.
Write down <u>two</u> advantages of using the orbit shown on the diagram.

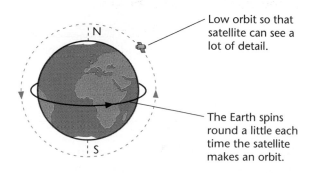

Low orbit so that satellite can see a lot of detail.

The Earth spins round a little each time the satellite makes an orbit.

1 Copy the grid below.
Write in the **bold** words that match the clues.
One has been done for you.

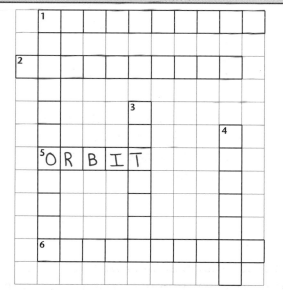

Across
1 Satellites put into their orbits by humans.
2 Satellites are put into orbit well above the Earth's
____.
5 Make up your own clue for this word.
6 Most of the other planets also have ____ in orbit around them.

Down
1 Scientists who study the stars are called ____.
3 The Moon is the Earth's ____ satellite.
4 Satellites can be used to look down on the Earth's
____.

5.7 What holds the solar system together?

Any two objects attract each other with a force that we call **gravity**.
For this force of gravity to be big enough to notice, one (or both) of the objects must have a very large mass.

Everything in the solar system is held in place by gravity.

The force of gravity between the **Sun** and each **planet** pulls the planet towards the Sun. But each planet also **moves** in a direction that would take it away from the Sun.

Together, these two effects keep each planet moving in its **orbit** around the Sun.

2 (a) Why is there a large force of gravity between the Earth and a satellite?

(b) A satellite orbits the Earth. Why doesn't the Earth orbit the satellite instead?

1 Copy the diagram. Add the sentences. Use the **bold** words to fill in the blanks.

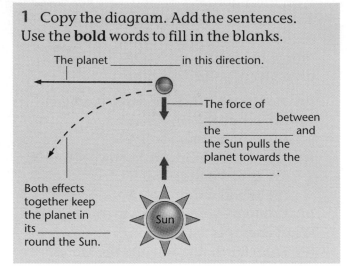

The planet _____ in this direction.

The force of _____ between the _____ and the Sun pulls the planet towards the _____ .

Both effects together keep the planet in its _____ round the Sun.

The force of gravity is the same size on both the Earth and the satellite. But it has a bigger effect on the satellite because it has a smaller mass.

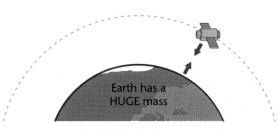

Earth has a HUGE mass

The force of gravity between two objects is very small unless one (or both) of the objects has a very large mass.

5.8 Why we need the Sun

Without energy from the **Sun**:

■ there would be no life on Earth:
plants need light energy from the Sun to grow and animals need plants for food.

■ there would be no weather:
energy from the Sun causes winds, it also evaporates water from the sea and this then falls as rain.

■ there would be far fewer energy sources:
● no coal or oil would have formed in the past;
● there would be no wood, no wind and no waves.

There would still be **geothermal** energy and **tides**. The Earth's crust would still contain the **uranium** that is used as a fuel in nuclear power stations.

Energy from the Sun has been reaching the Earth for nearly 5 billion years.

Scientists think that the Sun will keep shining much as it does today for about another 5 billion years.

1 Copy and complete the sentences.

Most of our energy sources depend in one way or another on the _____ .

Three energy sources that do not depend on the Sun are _____ , _____ and _____ .

2 The energy that the Sun sends out is produced by hydrogen being made into helium.
About how much of the Sun's hydrogen has already been made into helium?
Give a reason for your answer.